Grammar Power— the Essential Elements

Student Workbook

Curriculum Unit

Mary Louise Wanamaker

The Center for Learning

The Author

Mary Louise Wanamaker, who earned her M.A. at St. Louis University, has taught English, grades 9–12, to all ability levels. She concentrated on developing curriculum during her sixteen years as principal. Wanamaker also has twelve years' experience as a teacher supervisor at Province High Schools, Los Angeles, where she worked with principals on curriculum matters. She is the author of The Center for Learning's *Grammar Mastery—For Better Writing* workbooks and teacher guide.

The Publishing Team

Rose Schaffer, M.A., President/Chief Executive Officer
Bernadette Vetter, M.A., Vice President
Amy Hollis, B.S.J., Editor
Diana Culbertson, Ph.D., Editor

Cover Design

Susan Sheaffer Curtis, B.A.

ISBN 1-56077-593-9

Contents

Unit 8
Conjunctions and
Interjections

Supplementary Material

To the Students

Here it is at last: a workbook written just for you! It contains the basics of grammar that will prepare you for your English and foreign language courses in high school. It also lays the foundation for the mastery of writing skills, which is the primary purpose of any study of grammar.

This textbook is divided into units. The first unit teaches sentences, fragments, and the components of the simple sentence. The next seven units develop each part of speech with explanations and many exercises for reinforcement. The concepts in each unit prepare you for the next because all concepts are taught sequentially and there is much repetition and drill. If you don't master a concept at first, don't worry. You will grasp it in time!

The workbook also includes a section of exercises for words that often cause difficulty and confusion. While rules of punctuation and usage are included where they fit logically within a unit, some general punctuation rules and review exercises are located near the end of the workbook. The last section is a language drill that will prepare you for high school and help you master important concepts.

Grammar Power is a workbook that will give you power. It will not only adequately prepare you for high school, but it will also help you develop your ability to write well and correctly. Master the material one step at a time. This knowledge is of utmost importance. It will give you the self-confidence needed to tackle more complex structures as you continue your educational journey. May you be successful in all your endeavors. Keep working! Your future is in your hands.

Unit 1
Sentences

What Is a Sentence?

A **sentence** is a group of words that expresses a complete thought. A group of words is not a sentence unless it makes some kind of a statement, asks a question, gives a command or a request, or shows strong feeling. A complete sentence must have a topic or subject and a predicate that states what that subject is doing.

Exercise 1

Directions: Write complete statements using the following subjects.

Example: the calendar   *The calendar is on her desk.*

1. my math book

2. his little sister

3. the air in the room

4. the storm

5. his pencil

6. the bookcase in my room

7. her computer

8. the picture on the wall

9. the window in our classroom

10. the vase of flowers

11. Joe's car

12. the tornado

13. Bill

14. the evening news

15. her rose garden

Exercise 2

Directions: Add subjects to make the following groups of words complete sentences.

Example: *Her cousin* lives in the blue house.

1. _____ travels five miles each day.

2. _____ loves science.

3. _____ takes care of her little sister.

4. _____ went to the movies.

5. _____ needs stamps.

6. _____ will visit the Getty Museum.

7. _____ took the roof off our house.

8. _____ filed the papers on her desk.

9. _____ painted the bedroom.

10. _____ was an excellent artist.

Exercise 3

Directions: Write the letter of the group of words that logically completes the subject.

Example: She found the town   *k*

_____ 1.   The U.S. senator   a.   panned for gold.

_____ 2.   The librarian   b.   destroyed two city blocks.

_____ 3.   Travel agents   c.   went on a field trip.

_____ 4.   A gold miner   d.   grows in the ocean.

_____ 5.   The principal   e.   gave a talk on the importance of books.

_____ 6.   The tables   f.   were painted green and gold, the school colors.

_____ 7.   A tornado

_____ 8.   The children   g.   works in Washington, D.C.

_____ 9.   Kelp   h.   gave the class a free day.

_____ 10.   The U.S. Mint   i.   produces coins.

                                    j.   sell airline tickets.

                                    k.   on the map.

A **fragment** is a group of words that has either no subject, or no predicate, or does not express a complete thought.

> Flying a kite on a windy day in spring.

Who is flying the kite? There is no subject, so this is a fragment.

> John, an eighth-grade basketball player for Lincoln Junior High School and a talented student.

The topic is *John,* but we do not know what John is doing. It is a fragment.

> Listening carefully to every word spoken and every gesture given.

There is no subject or predicate. This is a fragment.

Exercise 4

Directions: If the group of words is a sentence, write *S.* If the words are not a sentence, mark *F.*

Example: When the clock strikes five. *F*

_____ 1.   The sun on that beautiful summer day.

_____ 2.   After the storm and after the cleanup.

_____ 3.   My friend is going to Hawaii next summer.

_____ 4.   Early in the morning before the sun had dried the mist on the grass,

_____ 5.   Write your name at the top of the papers.

_____ 6.   On the dusty road traveled by so many people.

_____ 7.   Jane wants to become a teacher.

_____ 8.   Our team won the game last night.

_____ 9.   The motto written on the blackboard for everyone to see.

_____ 10.   Bill hurt his arm playing soccer.

_____ 11.   Stop immediately!

_____ 12.   Working day and night for a minimum wage.

_____ 13.   Leaving his dog with his friend to go on a trip.

_____ 14.   Jean bought her first car, a Volvo.

_____ 15.   Pay attention!

_____ 16.   Jim won second place on the game show.

_____ 17.   This year there were many storms and tornadoes.

_____ 18.   There are millions of insects after a wet winter.

_____ 19.   The beauty of the woods and the sunsets.

_____ 20.   Enjoying his vacation at the beach.

Dependent Clauses

Exercise 5

A group of words can have a subject and a predicate, and not express a complete thought. These are **dependent clauses**; they depend on another clause to give them meaning.

Before Jack picked up the marbles.

The subject is *Jack*; the predicate is *picked*, but this clause does not express a complete thought. It needs another clause to complete its meaning.

Directions: If the group of words expresses a complete thought, write *C*. If the words do not express a complete thought, write *N*.

Example: Last week after school *N*

_____ 1. He joined his brother on the tennis courts.

_____ 2. If you want to go on an exciting ride down the rapids.

_____ 3. Although Tom was a good student who did his homework regularly.

_____ 4. Write carefully but do not print.

_____ 5. The class did not understand the problem.

_____ 6. After you choose your teams and after you give each member a particular job.

_____ 7. If you want to become a member of our debating team.

_____ 8. When you decide to write your final report and give it to your coach.

_____ 9. Camping overnight in Pine Valley and watching the sun set over the lake, we watched in wonder.

_____ 10. It seems wiser to ignore him.

_____ 11. Eating his lunch hurriedly, James ran out to the baseball diamond.

_____ 12. After the team won the game and long before the celebration began.

_____ 13. We watched the game on our TV.

_____ 14. Although Ted was ill with a very bad cold.

_____ 15. When do you plan to return from your vacation?

_____ 16. Who sent in this article?

_____ 17. Since my brother lost his job at Taco Bell.

_____ 18. While you were enjoying yourself at Tom's party last night.

_____ 19. Jerry's wallet, a birthday gift, was lost last week at the game.

_____ 20. While my sister and I cleaned our rooms and vacuumed.

_____ 21. If you are planning to enter the science contest, please let me know as soon as possible.

_____ 22. Alice left without permission.

_____ 23. That you assumed full responsibility for the incident.

_____ 24. He did not plan to go to the basketball game.

_____ 25. Since everyone agreed with his proposal.

Run-on Sentences

When a comma joins two complete sentences, the incorrect result is a **run-on sentence**. (One sentence runs on into the next.)

> Mark Twain is a good storyteller, he knows how to keep his reader in suspense.

The comma joins the two complete sentences and makes it an incorrect run-on sentence.

A run-on sentence can also occur when there is no punctuation between sentences.

> Jack plays baseball his little sister likes tennis.

Run-on sentences can be corrected in several ways. These will be studied later, but you should be able to recognize run-on sentences and avoid using them.

Exercise 6

Directions: Write _F_ for a fragment, _R_ for a run-on sentence, or _S_ for a sentence.

Example: The artist bought a new paintbrush. _S_

_____ 1. A beautiful sunrise on a winter's day.

_____ 2. The new museum displayed many beautiful paintings.

_____ 3. Carefully arranging the flowers in their vases.

_____ 4. Chuck plays the cello well he also plays in the band.

_____ 5. Eating his lunch every day in the school cafeteria.

_____ 6. The TV given to her on her birthday.

_____ 7. The news of winning the championship made us all happy.

_____ 8. Did you read the article in the newspaper it gave our girls' basketball team a lot of praise.

_____ 9. After the storm we surveyed the damage.

_____ 10. During the game we cheered enthusiastically our volleyball team is the best in the city.

_____ 11. You should leave the room in good condition.

_____ 12. Give me your telephone number.

_____ 13. Turning on the light and walking cautiously.

_____ 14. A science club was started this year, instead of just reading the material we can now do science experiments.

_____ 15. Meet me in the gym.

_____ 16. It will probably rain on the weekend don't do too much planning.

_____ 17. Count your blessings.

_____ 18. Trying hard to receive honors in math in June.

_____ 19. Paul is one of our best players he should plan to join the team in high school.

_____ 20. Did you get all the problems right which ones were the most difficult?

_____ 21. I'm leaving now.

_____ 22. There is too much violence on TV something should be done.

_____ 23. Report for your physical exam here.

_____ 24. Her ability to write was the key to her success, she was also very bright.

_____ 25. Everyone seemed to enjoy the musical, the comments, however, were not always favorable.

Exercise 7

Directions: Write *F* for a fragment, *DC* for a dependent clause, *R* for a run-on, or *S* for a sentence.

Example: Although you left early.   *DC*

_____ 1. Before he was able to contact his boss.

_____ 2. Ray shot the winning basket last night, he won the game.

_____ 3. After you write your composition and proofread it.

_____ 4. Lois couldn't find her library card.

_____ 5. Sitting in the booth waiting for her father to join her.

_____ 6. A cold wintry morning with patches of snow everywhere.

_____ 7. Send us the recipe.

_____ 8. Since you have borrowed books from our library on a weekly basis.

_____ 9. Gloria learned about the party on Thursday she already had other plans.

_____ 10. Because there was nothing she could do about the problem.

_____ 11. Larry's hobby, saving stamps especially from Asiatic countries.

_____ 12. Before the tornado touched ground in our town.

_____ 13. Always do your best.

_____ 14. Unless you are willing to give me the material that I need to finish my project.

_____ 15. As a class we visited the zoo in San Diego last week.

_____ 16. The wind whirling leaves around our front porch.

_____ 17. She decided to write her autobiography at least she thought she would write it.

_____ 18. Entering the darkened auditorium about an hour before the concert would begin.

_____ 19. Cats are very interesting, they pretend they don't need any affection.

_____ 20. Working several problems in his math book to show the teacher he understood the material.

Sentence Functions

There are four sentence functions: declarative, interrogative, imperative, and exclamatory.

1. *Declarative*—makes a statement and ends with a period

> John is going to college next fall.
>
> Carol received the award for best tennis player.
>
> A storm caused much damage in the South.

2. *Interrogative*—asks a question and ends with a question mark

> Where did you put my books?
>
> Are you going on the field trip with the class?
>
> Do you like sports?

To find the subject of an interrogative sentence, rearrange the sentence to make it declarative.

> Did Tom bring the drinks?
>
> Tom did bring the drinks.

3. *Imperative*—gives a command or makes a request and ends with a period or exclamation

> (You) wash the dishes.
>
> (You) please leave the room.
>
> Will you please give me that pen.

Do not use a question mark with a request.

4. *Exclamatory*—expresses strong feeling and ends with an exclamation mark

Watch out!

Help!

Leave that vase alone!

Exercise 8

Directions: Label the following sentences *D* for declarative, *IN* for interrogative, *IM* for imperative, or *E* for exclamatory. Then add the correct end punctuation.

Example: Do you know what time the game starts *IN* ?

_____ 1. He is leaving for Africa tomorrow

_____ 2. Finish your math problems tonight

_____ 3. What did you watch on TV last night

_____ 4. Such a remark is insulting

_____ 5. Do you think it will rain tomorrow

_____ 6. Please help me with my homework

_____ 7. Throw those towels in the basket

_____ 8. We went to the game last night

_____ 9. Will you please clean your room

_____ 10. Look out

_____ 11. What happened to your English book

_____ 12. The school bought fifty new computers

_____ 13. Technology is helping students

_____ 14. There will be a meeting of coaches

_____ 15. There's no time to lose

_____ 16. Where are you putting the flowers

_____ 17. The building is in flames

_____ 18. Did you see the comet

_____ 19. This heat is unbearable

_____ 20. Close the window

_____ 21. The principal gave a talk last night

_____ 22. Watch where you're going

_____ 23. Please iron your blouse

_____ 24. Is this your book

_____ 25. Three cheers for Sally

Simple and Complete Subjects

The simple subject is the main word of the complete subject. Words or phrases that modify the simple subject form the complete subject.

Several large boxes of tomatoes were picked yesterday.

This sentence is talking about boxes. The boxes are several, large with tomatoes.

A red truck passed our house.

This sentence is talking about a truck. It is red.

The seventh grade boys in my homeroom had a debate.

This sentence is talking about boys. They are in the seventh grade and are in my homeroom.

My class in mathematics is working on a math project.

Class / in mathematics
Simple subject / modifies the simple subject

Bob   gave a science demonstration.
Simple subject

There are no modifiers, so *Bob* is also the complete subject.

Our eighth grade went roller skating on Saturday.

Grade is the simple subject. The complete subject is *our eighth grade.*

Exercise 9

Directions: Underline the subjects in the following phrases.

Example: the large <u>apartment</u> near my house

1. brown beach towel

2. two colored blankets

3. large bottles of Pepsi

4. a playpen with toys

5. the tiny stream of water

6. a bag of cookies

7. a beautiful Monarch butterfly

8. a bottle of aspirin

9. a visit to the country

10. a large beautiful mansion

11. a little child's rocking chair

12. a girl's skirt

13. a bundle of papers

9

14. several toy dogs

15. a flock of birds

16. a shelf of books

17. a couple of clowns

18. a history of England

19. several new vans

20. a tiny white bunny

Notes

a.   A prepositional phrase is never the subject.

   A bag of groceries was standing on the kitchen sink.

The simple subject is *bag*. The complete subject is *a bag of groceries.*

b.   *There* and *here* often come first in a sentence, but they are never subjects.

   There they sat for two hours.

The subject is *they.*

   Here are the boxes.

The subject is *boxes.*

c.   In most declarative sentences the subject comes first. This is called *normal order*. Sometimes the subject is preceded by a phrase or modifier. This is called *inverted word order.*

   Near the mall stood a bewildered little boy.

In interrogative sentences the subject is between parts of the verb.

   Why did Jim leave so quickly?

In imperative sentences the subject is usually you understood.

   Take this to the store.

   Give me that paper.

Exercise 10

Directions: Underline the simple subject in the following list of complete subjects.

Example: a <u>story</u> in my favorite book

1.   the desk in my room

2.   a little stray black cat

3.   a bag of cookies

4.   the baseball bat on the porch

5.   a child's book of poetry

6.   a trunk of clothes

7.   a glass of milk

8.   a survey of the land

9. five gallons of gas

10. a basket of fruit

11. ten bottles of glue

12. several cans of soup

13. two business letters

14. a delicious chocolate cake

15. a banana cream pie

16. a stack of papers

17. big ferocious bulldog

18. a skating rink with children

19. beautiful flowers of many colors

20. a tall vase of flowers

Exercise 11

Directions: Add simple subjects to make your own sentences.

Example: Our softball _____ needs a pitcher. *team*

1. A _____ of cookies was in my lunch.

2. Several _____ of coffee were on the table.

3. A _____ with her kittens was sunning herself on the porch.

4. My _____ loves to play tennis.

5. Her new IBM _____ was broken.

6. Rich chocolate _____ covered the cake.

7. Many colored _____ were sold at the circus.

8. A couple of_____ were skating on the rink.

9. A beautiful _____ crossed the sky after the storm.

10. My strawberry ice cream _____ tastes delicious.

Exercise 12

Directions: Underline the simple subject.

Example: My younger <u>brother</u> plays the piano well.

1. A furry little dog ran into our yard.

2. A beautiful picture of a brook and trees hangs in our room.

3. The boy driving the truck hauls groceries each morning.

4. The desk in my bedroom was made by my father.

5. Several get-well cards were sent to the invalid.

6. The walls in our hallway need a coat of paint.

7. The news of the accident arrived yesterday.

8. The terrible storm caused much damage.

9. A carton of milk stood on the counter.

10. A bottle of vinegar fell on the clean kitchen floor.

11. Here comes the football team!

12. Our class enjoyed the play.

13. Our beautiful lace tablecloth was torn.

14. A raging fire destroyed my sister's house.

15. Our best soccer player broke his arm.

16. Our football team won the game.

17. There in the driveway lay a bat and a glove.

18. The rally for the final game was held on Thursday.

19. Tom's backpack was stolen.

20. The school's newspaper received a special award.

21. The clock in our kitchen stopped.

22. Coming down the street were my two friends.

23. On the kitchen table was a vase of roses.

24. After eating quickly, Sally dashed out of the house.

25. Computers have taken the place of typewriters.

Directions: Underline the complete subject and put parentheses around the simple subject.

Example: The top (students) in the class visited the Huntington Library.

1. The rain flooded the streets.

2. A dish of grapes was on the table in the patio.

3. Two cans of tomato soup sat on the empty shelf.

4. The football coach with his assistants was given directions.

5. A shelf of snacks was a popular meeting place in our house.

6. A packet of library cards was given to the librarian.

7. Early each morning Jane runs two miles in the park.

8. The cart with many boxes was left in the hall.

9. Happy with the outcome of his test, Carl telephoned his mother.

10. Stop before you act!

11. Joe, as well as his brothers, is going to the beach on Saturday.

12. The magazines were put on the shelf in the library.

13. On the table were several plates of pizza.

14. The coach for the school's basketball team is a graduate of USC.

15. Jerry's father plays the guitar.

16. Not one of the students was prepared for the test.

17. Each of the girls in the room received an A.

18. Mary's mother coaches our volleyball team.

19. Always put your best foot forward.

20. Her courage in the face of danger was impressive.

Compound Subjects

When there are two or more subjects in a sentence, the subject is compound.

Mario and his brother go to the same school.

In this sentence *Mario* and *his brother* is the subject of the sentence.

Directions: Underline the simple compound subjects.

Example: The dog and the cat ran down the street.

1. The White House and the Pentagon called a press conference.

2. A typewriter and a computer were in her office.

3. The doctors and nurses attended a meeting on Tuesday.

4. Milk, butter, and cheese were placed on the table.

5. Bob and Carlos won the first prize in the science competition.

6. Many flowers and plants depend on insects for growth.

7. Moths or beetles can destroy clothes.

8. Bees and ants can ruin a picnic.

9. Girls and boys must obey the rules.

10. The rivers and lakes were flooded during the storm.

Appositives

An **appositive** renames the noun that it follows.

> John, my friend, enjoys tennis.

Friend is an appositive of *John*.

Appositives help to reduce wordiness in writing. Always separate appositives with commas.

> John enjoys tennis. He is my friend.
>
> *John, my friend, enjoys tennis.*
>
> Jerry, student body president, gave a speech yesterday.

The subject is *Jerry*. The appositive (or apposition) to the subject is *student body president*.

Exercise 15

Directions: Add appositives to the following nouns. Punctuate correctly.

Example: Garrett, *an inventor,*

1. Miss Brown _____

2. My father _____

3. The president _____

4. Pete _____

5. Our dog _____

6. The Wizard of Oz _____

7. Magic Johnson _____

8. My little sister _____

9. The best student in our class _____

10. Thomas Edison _____

Directions: Use appositives to combine the thoughts in each pair of sentences.

Example: Molly Blair is a cheerleader. She is also a top student in her class.

Molly Blair, a cheerleader, is also a top student in her class.

1. Lee Hutchins is an early riser. He invented the alarm clock.

2. Bob is a good basketball player. He is the editor of the school paper.

3. Chuck won the student council election. He is popular with all the students.

4. Barb won the lead in the school play. She is a born actor.

5. Marie loves music. She sings in the school's choir.

6. Jane is a teacher in India. She enjoys teaching the young students to read.

7. Molly works with computers. She is a math genius.

8. Mark Twain is a great storyteller. He enjoyed entertaining others with his tales.

9. Sally made the costumes for the school play. She is an excellent seamstress.

10. Dr. Martin Luther King, Jr., fought for human rights. He was an outstanding speaker.

11. Michael Jordan played baseball. He is noted as a basketball player.

12. John F. Kennedy was assassinated in Dallas. He was president of the United States.

13. Janet was born in Canada. She is now a citizen of the United States.

14. Leo is our class president. He is an exceptional leader.

15. Lois is a lover of nature. She is also an advocate for the environment.

16. Al painted a mural on the school wall. He is an exceptional artist.

17. Bob qualified for the golf tournament. He is now a professional.

18. Lisa is an efficient administrator. She is taking a new job next year.

19. The *Titanic* sank in 1912. It was on its maiden voyage.

20. Joan works as an accountant. She received a promotion last week.

Simple and Complete Predicates

Simple Predicate

The **simple predicate** of a sentence is the verb. It tells what the subject is doing or what is being done to the subject.

> Bob played football in the park with his friends.

Bob is the subject. The sentence is about Bob.

Played is the verb, or simple predicate. It tells what Bob did.

> Bob played.

> My friends and I enjoyed the concert.

Friends, I is the compound subject. The sentence is about friends and I.

Enjoyed is the verb, or simple predicate. It tells what the subject did.

> Friends and I enjoyed.

Exercise 17

Directions: Underline the simple predicates in the following sentences. Remember, the predicate tells what the subject is doing.

Example: Gloria <u>sings</u> in the choir.

1. Terry laughed at the joke.

2. My brother works in that store.

3. Our teacher also plays the piano.

4. A group of girls visited an orphanage in Mexico.

5. My brother varnished the table.

6. Jim plays soccer.

7. Tom swims every morning.

8. Julie studies computer literacy.

9. My sister returned the book to the library.

10. The orange rolled under the table.

11. Jane dusted the chairs in the room.

12. Jerry's father strummed the guitar.

13. Joe runs five miles every day.

14. The students cheered for their team.

15. My uncle works for my father.

16. A flock of pigeons snatched our lunches.

17. A raging fire destroyed my sister's house.

18. Last night we counted the loose change.

19. Sally studied ballet for five years.

20. The Gillis Construction Company built four schools.

Exercise 18

Directions: Write the simple subject and the simple predicate for each of the sentences in **Exercise 17**.

Example: Gloria sings in the choir. *Gloria sings.*

Complete Predicate

The verb is always the simple predicate. The verb and its modifiers form the **complete predicate**.

> John earned an A in math.

The simple predicate *earned* tells what John did.
The modifiers are *an A in math.*

> Kate won a scholarship to high school.

What did Kate do? She won.
Won is the simple predicate. *A scholarship to high school* modifies *won* and completes the predicate.

> Dave jogs every morning.

Jogs is the simple predicate. *Every* and *morning* are modifiers of the predicate and form the complete predicate.

Exercise 19

Directions: Underline the simple predicate and put parentheses around the complete predicate.

Example: Our team (<u>practices</u>) after school every night.

1. Tony found a wallet on the street.

2. Sally practices her violin every evening for one hour.

3. Terry wrote and published the store's bulletin.

4. The manager praised Terry for her work and gave her a raise.

5. The wind blew down several small houses.

6. Joe ordered pizza for the entire team.

7. My brother played in the rain.

8. Carl enjoys football but plays on the basketball team.

9. Tom's father coaches the school's soccer team.

10. Pat's picture won first place in the art contest.

11. Write carefully and check for mistakes.

12. The dog ran to my friend's house and sat on the porch.

13. The teacher praised Laura for her essay and gave her an A.

14. Each of the students placed the papers on the teacher's desk.

15. The principal promised a rally for the next volleyball game.

16. The driver of the truck lost control and plowed into a van.

17. Emma had never seen snow.

18. Maria washes and sets her hair each morning.

19. The policeman visited the school and talked with the students.

20. Judy teaches primary grades at Clark Elementary School.

Directions: Underline the simple subject or subjects and put parentheses around the simple predicate. Note that the simple predicate may be composed of more than one word.

Example: Where *(did)* <u>you</u> *(put)* my lunch?

1. The electricians worked long and hard after the storm.

2. Both Paige and Riley won a trip to Washington, D.C.

3. Did Pete and Kathy enjoy the concert last night?

4. The material in the test gave me a headache.

5. The cover of the magazine was torn.

6. Did the teacher accept Peggy's excuse?

7. Everyone enjoyed the trip to Disneyland.

8. The pictures in my sister's book were pretty.

9. The waves damaged the pier.

10. Eat your lunch slowly.

11. Terry washes her hands often.

12. The people in the doctor's office fidgeted nervously.

13. The children stood in line for more than thirty minutes.

14. The cookies made the children happy.

15. A bag of popcorn was given to each student.

16. Did you see the plate of doughnuts on the table?

17. One of the tickets for the Lakers game this evening was lost.

18. Several pieces of cloth were torn from the material.

19. That picture of our Halloween costumes gave my little sister nightmares.

20. Her jokes make me laugh.

21. Two pairs of shoes were found in the gym after the volleyball game last night.

22. My little sister can count to one hundred.

23. Jean, my oldest sister, and I have seen that show three times.

24. The noise during the rally made my ears ache.

25. The bottle of perfume broke and filled the house with a pleasant smell.

Directions: Write the simple subject and simple predicate of the following sentences.

Example: A picture of my mother stood on my desk.   *picture stood*

1.   His dog takes a walk every morning and evening.

2.   My computer broke last night.

3.   Pete will go with you tomorrow.

4.   The attorney sent the letter.

5.   The globe stood on a stand.

6.   The cherries ripened early this year.

7.   My father planted carrots and onions in our garden.

8.   My friend helped me with my homework.

9.   My little sister gave a piercing scream.

10. Jerry took pictures of our party.

11. His father cut out the newspaper article.

12. My mother vacuumed the rug.

13. Tim threw stones into the lake.

14. Our class went to the Museum of Fine Arts.

15. Bob plays games on his computer.

16. Brian tore his coat on the fence.

17. Mary scrubbed each chair carefully.

18. A glass of orange juice spilled onto my composition.

19. Jane straightened the chairs in the room.

20. Joe, my brother, damaged our car.

Compound Predicates

Directions: Find ten simple sentences from a story you are reading. Write each sentence and underline its simple subject and simple predicate.

A **compound predicate** consists of two or more verbs joined by a conjunction and having the same subject.

> Tina ran into her room and slammed the door.

The subject is *Tina*. The compound predicates are *ran* and *slammed*.

Compound predicates often help to reduce wordiness.

> Toby, our cat, sat on the windowsill. He sunned himself.
> *Toby, our cat, sat on the windowsill and sunned himself.*

Directions: Use compound predicates to combine each pair of sentences.

Example: We went to the store. We bought oranges. *We went to the store and bought oranges.*

1. My Uncle Joe visits us every Thanksgiving. He always brings the dessert.

2. My brother plays in a band. He sings with great enthusiasm.

3. Jake and I enjoy our summer. We ride bikes. We also swim in the lake.

4. Our football team won the final game. We earned the first-place trophy.

5. Her cat Corky likes to play games. He hides in the bushes and trees.

6. Our family went to the mountains. We climbed the trails. We barbecued on an outdoor grill.

7. On her vacation, Jenny wrote letters to her friends. She sent little home-made gifts to her mother.

8. Patty vacuumed her room. She straightened the books in the bookcase. She picked up papers and magazines. She dusted the furniture.

9. My mother grows tomatoes and onions in her garden. She also cultivates beautiful roses.

10. Marian worked conscientiously in school. She did her homework every night.

11. The little girl ran and jumped in the park. She also swung on the swings. She played in the sand box.

12. Mary gave the homeless man a sandwich and an apple. She also found a comfortable place for him to rest.

13. Jan washed all the desks in the classroom. She cleaned the chalkboards. She also dusted the bookcases.

14. Becky lifted the lid off the box. She found a bracelet and a pair of earrings.

15. Patty visited her aunt and uncle in Florida. She flew to Hawaii for a week's vacation with her best friend.

16. Ants crawled all over the sink in my bathroom. They covered my bottle of shampoo. They even ate the sugar coating on my Advil pills.

17. Jerry, wash your hands thoroughly. Set the table for dinner.

18. My father read the newspaper. He smoked his nightly cigar. He then fell asleep.

19. Paul opened the front door cautiously and quietly. He tiptoed upstairs. He opened his bedroom door. He jumped into bed.

20. Every Saturday John cuts the grass. He pulls out the weeds. He sweeps the sidewalks.

Unit 1
Unit 1 Review

1. Every sentence must express a complete thought. It must have a subject and a predicate. The subject is what the sentence is about. The predicate tells what the subject is, was, or will be doing. Sometimes the predicate tells what is, was, or will be done to the subject.

2. A fragment never expresses a complete thought. Often fragments are missing a subject or a predicate or both.

3. Dependent clauses have a subject and a predicate, but they do not express a complete thought.

4. A run-on sentence has two or more sentences joined by a comma, or with no punctuation.

5. There are four sentence functions:

    a. declarative
    makes a statement

    b. interrogative
    asks a question

    c. imperative
    gives a command or makes a request

    d. exclamatory
    expresses strong feelings

6. The subject of a sentence tells who or what the sentence is about. The modifiers and the simple subject make up the complete subject. The simple subject is never part of a prepositional phrase.

7. The predicate often tells what the subject is doing. The simple predicate is the verb. The complete predicate is the verb and its modifiers.

8. Compound predicates have more than one verb. They often help reduce wordiness.

9. Appositives rename the nouns they follow. Appositives are set off by commas.

Unit 1
Review Test

Part A.

Directions: Write *S* for sentence or *F* for fragment.

_____ 1. Enjoying the gentle evening breeze on that hot day.

_____ 2. Eat your lunch early today.

_____ 3. Look before you act.

_____ 4. The road, dusty and hot, in late autumn.

_____ 5. Sitting quietly by the lake trying to catch a fish.

_____ 6. Did you finish the assignment?

24

_____ 7. Jake earned his letter in baseball.

_____ 8. On the road leading to town.

_____ 9. Send Tom the bill.

_____ 10. When will you graduate from college?

Part B.

Directions: If the group of words is a sentence, write _S_. If it is a run-on sentence, write _R_. If it has a subject and predicate but does not express a complete thought, write _N_.

_____ 1. Although Roger is a very good student, always willing to help out when needed.

_____ 2. Albert is always willing to accept advice.

_____ 3. John is going to take computer science he is a whiz with computers.

_____ 4. Mabel works with her mother during the summer she is an excellent organizer.

_____ 5. Before you write your composition tonight.

_____ 6. At the meeting we all formed a circle and joined hands, we then sang the school song.

_____ 7. Before my brother gets ready to go to a party or to a game.

_____ 8. A snake slithered into our parlor, crawled up on the windowsill, and rested there quietly.

_____ 9. If you all agree with my proposal and if you get permission from your parents in time.

_____ 10. Larry, my friend, was hit by a car and was taken to the hospital, he was released that same day.

Part C.

Directions: Underline the simple subject and put parentheses around the simple predicate.

1. On the side of the road stood a tall pine tree.

2. Write your name on the bottom line.

3. After jumping into every puddle, my brother was completely wet.

4. Jack and Muriel, his sister, go to the same school.

5. A bag of groceries was sitting on the table.

6. Ice and snow can cause accidents.

7. A can of beans was open on the counter.

8. Every little thing can often bring happiness.

9. The accident happened early in the morning.

10. Each of the papers was ruined by rain.

11. On the corner of the desk stood a small statue.

12. Jon broke his ankle in the game last night.

13. Wind and rain caused havoc to the trees on our street.

14. Bill, the quarterback, is going to USC.

15. Marlene was chosen the editor of the school paper.

16. Shivering in the cold, Jerry quickly delivered his papers.

17. The boys in our class gave twenty dollars to help a poor family.

18. Are there any more letters in the box?

19. Marilyn always does her homework.

20. Go immediately to the gym after lunch.

Part D.

Directions: Label the following sentences *D* for declarative, *IN* for interrogative, *IM* for imperative, or *E* for exclamatory. Then add correct end punctuation.

_____ 1. Stop when you see a train

_____ 2. The county received more than four inches of rain

_____ 3. Did you do your homework last night

_____ 4. Watch out or you'll get hurt

_____ 5. Clean your room now

_____ 6. Did you watch the game last night

_____ 7. Are there any more letters in the box

_____ 8. Joyce won first place in both races

_____ 9. Kenneth will visit the White House

_____ 10. Mary joined the French Club

Part E.

Directions: Write appositives for the following subjects. Punctuate correctly.

1. Sally _____ won the race.

2. Mr. Jones _____ will move to Oregon.

3. George _____ saved the game.

4. Joann _____ will go to the Olympics.

5. Sydney _____ has a large bushy tail.

6. The storm _____ cost millions in damages.

7. Her cousin _____ is a good basketball player.

8. *Titanic* _____ grossed over a billion dollars.

9. Paul's mother _____ is involved in school activities.

10. Our teacher _____ enjoys teaching.

Part F.

Directions: Combine each pair of sentences by using appositives. Punctuate correctly.

1. Ginny enjoys traveling. She is my mothers' cousin.

2. Miss Jones has been my teacher for two years. She was a math major at Georgetown University.

3. George has a great love for classical music. He plays the violin and the cello.

4. Stella wants to be an actress. She studies drama in college.

5. Jerry is studying to be a mechanic. He enjoys working with all models of cars.

What Is a Noun?

A **noun** is the name of a person, place, thing, or idea.

James	person
Mount Baldy	place
computer	thing
justice	idea

Exercise 24

Directions: Write whether the underlined noun is a person, place, thing, or idea.

Example: My <u>watch</u> is broken. *thing*

_____ 1. His <u>house</u> was destroyed by a tornado.

_____ 2. My <u>computer</u> saves me many hours of work.

_____ 3. <u>Teachers</u> must love to teach.

_____ 4. My brother and I visited the <u>Smithsonian Institute</u>.

_____ 5. <u>Disneyland</u> is a popular vacation destination.

_____ 6. Paul wanted the <u>truth</u>.

_____ 7. Her <u>roses</u> are beautiful.

_____ 8. <u>Mary Pierce</u> is a great tennis player.

_____ 9. Our library has many reference <u>books</u>.

_____ 10. Todd's <u>pride</u> was hurt.

Kinds of Nouns

Common Nouns

A **common noun** names any person, place, thing, or idea. (Hint: A noun is any word that you can put *the* in front of.)

lady	meat
dish	reward

Proper Nouns

A **proper noun** names a particular person, place, or thing.

Mr. Jones	Memorial Stadium	Atlantic Ocean

Abstract Nouns

An **abstract noun** names a quality or idea.

truth	beauty
pride	danger

Note

Nouns can be classified in more than one way. Sometimes abstract nouns can also be proper nouns.

Exercise 25

Directions: Label the following nouns *C* for common, *P* for proper, or *A* for abstract.

Example: map *C*

_____ 1.   Peter

_____ 2.   patriotism

_____ 3.   Japan

_____ 4.   wisdom

_____ 5.   Antarctic

_____ 6.   Yosemite National Park

_____ 7.   Ganges River

_____ 8.   hate

_____ 9.   Todd Miller

_____ 10.   street

_____ 11.   Aunt Jane

_____ 12.   comet

_____ 13.   success

_____ 14.   quarterback

_____ 15.   train

_____ 16.   rocking chair

_____ 17.   water

_____ 18.   Hot Springs

_____ 19.   desk

_____ 20.   Pierpont Inn

Capitalization of Proper Nouns

1. Proper nouns are capitalized.

> Dr. Marie Jerkins   Paul Jones   Terry Smith

2. Capitalize titles that come before a person's name or that take the place of a person's name.

> Uncle George   President Ford   Chief of Police

3. Do not capitalize *the, in, of,* or *a* unless they are the first word in a title.

> The Legend of Sleepy Hollow
>
> Of Mice and Men
>
> A Tale of Two Cities

4. Capitalize proper nouns that name specific regions of the country. Do not capitalize directions or seasons.

> We will visit the South this summer.
>
> We drove north on the freeway.
>
> Last summer we went to the beach.

Note

Generally an article precedes a specific part of the country.

Exercise 26

Directions: Write proper nouns for the following common nouns. Capitalize correctly.

Example: month   *June*

1. mountain   _____

2. movie   _____

3. street   _____

4. holiday   _____

5. club   _____

6. language   _____

7. freeway   _____

8. park   _____

9. monument   _____

10. museum   _____

11. city   _____

12. state   _____

13. arena   _____

14. high school   _____

15. grade school   _____

16. baseball park   _____

17. lake   _____

18. teacher   _____

19. principal   _____

20. river   _____

21. boy's name   _____

22. church   _____

23. football player   _____

24. basketball player   _____

25. girl's name   _____

Exercise 27

Directions: On a separate piece of paper, rewrite the following paragraph with correct capitalization.

My father, mother, and I visited the yellowstone national park in august. This park is the largest and oldest unit in the national park system of the united states. It is administered by the national park service. Park headquarters are located at mammoth, wyoming. Yellowstone has cut one of the great canyons of north america, over one thousand feet deep and twenty-four miles long. We were especially fascinated with the geysers. Approximately two hundred geysers have been observed and named. The most famous one we visited is old faithful, which is unusual especially for the height of its eruptions. It often shoots hot water over one hundred feet and sometimes even two hundred feet in the air. Even our visit to washington dc was not as spectacular. If you have never visited yellowstone national park, plan to go someday.

Exercise 28

Directions: Write a paragraph about a place you have visited. Include details about where it is located, when you visited it, and what interested you the most.

Singular and Plural Nouns

Singular Nouns

A **singular noun** names only one person, place, thing, or idea.

sister	school
chair	joy

Plural Nouns

A **plural noun** names more than one person, place, thing, or idea.

sisters	schools
chairs	joys

1. To form the plural of most singular nouns, add *s*.

grape	grapes
house	houses
apple	apples

2. To form the plural of nouns ending with *ch, sh, ss, z,* or *x,* add *es*.

church	churches
glass	glasses
tax	taxes
bus	buses

3. To form the plural of nouns ending in *y* preceded by a consonant, change the *y* to *i* and add *es*.

army	armies
lady	ladies
party	parties

4. To form the plural of nouns ending with *y* preceded by a vowel, add *s*.

donkey	donkeys
day	days
boy	boys

5. For a letter or a numeral, add *s*.

x	xs
b	bs
100	100s

6. To form the plural of a noun ending in *o*, add *s* or *es*.

piano	pianos
zero	zeroes
potato	potatoes

7. To form the plural of some nouns ending in *f* or *fe*, change the *f* or *fe* to *ve* and add *s*. For others, simply add *s*.

loaf	loaves
life	lives

chief	chiefs
safe	safes

8. Some singular nouns change form in the plural.

man	men
child	children
ox	oxen
woman	women

9. Some singular nouns are the same in the singular and the plural.

deer	deer
sheep	sheep
trout	trout

Compound Nouns

Compound nouns are made up of more than one word. Often compound nouns are separated by a hyphen. The main word in a compound nouns is made plural.

sister-in-law	sisters-in-law
great-grandfather	great-grandfathers
man-of-war	men-of-war

Exercise 29

Directions: Write the plural of the following nouns.

Example: key *keys*

1. street _____

2. knife _____

3. bunch _____

4. 1,000 _____

5. bevy _____

6. moose _____

7. box _____

8. match _____

9. hour _____

10. video _____

11. goose _____

12. hero _____

13. mother-in-law _____

14. life _____

15. monkey _____

16. bus _____

17. bench _____

18. built-in-helper _____

19. sister-in-law _____

20. D _____

Uses of a Noun

Nouns have different uses in a sentence.

Subject

The **subject** of a sentence is always a noun or a pronoun. (A pronoun can take the place of a noun.) The subject is a noun because the subject tells what the sentence is about. Subjects can be simple or compound.

> The hill collapsed during the rain storm.

In this sentence, *hill* is the simple subject.

> The wind and the rain caused much damage.

In this sentence, *wind* and *rain* are the compound subjects.

> The cars on the street were submerged in water.

In this sentence, the complete subject is *the cars on the street.* The simple subject is *cars.* Cars are what the sentence is about. *Cars* is a noun subject. The noun *street* follows a preposition. It is not the subject.

> A box of oranges was delivered yesterday.

The complete subject is *a box of oranges.* The simple subject is *box. Of oranges* is a phrase.

Exercise 30

Directions: Underline the simple subjects of the following sentences. Put parentheses around words that are part of the complete subject.

Example: (The carton of soap) was shipped to Africa.

1. A can of peaches was on the shelf.

2. Both Tom and Jerry made the team.

3. The bottle of vinegar was broken.

4. The pattern for the dress was given to me.

5. The money in that drawer belongs to my brother.

6. The doctor and the nurses volunteered their services.

7. The doctor, as well as the nurses, volunteered his service.

8. The professor of physics received an award from the university.

9. The entire shelf of books fell.

10. An army of ants invaded our kitchen last night.

11. The letter and the article were used as evidence.

12. The glass of milk by her bed was knocked over.

13. The entire crop of strawberries was destroyed by the storm.

14. Pat bought a computer yesterday.

15. The teachers, as well as the counselor, went with us to Disneyland.

16. A cloud of dust made driving dangerous.

17. The principal and the faculty enjoyed a short vacation.

18. A mixture of oil and molasses covered the sink.

19. Residents of the town celebrated the victory of their team.

20. The water under the bridge was contaminated.

Apposition to the Subject (Appositive)

The **apposition to the subject** (the appositive) is the same as the subject. An appositive renames any noun it follows. Appositives are set off by commas.

> Tony, a champion skater, won a scholarship.

Tony is the noun subject; *Skater* is in apposition to Tony, stating what Tony is.

A compound appositive is two or more appositives or appositive phrases that identify the same noun

> Our vacation, a weekend in Yosemite National Park and a week in Hawaii, brought us many exciting experiences.

Exercise 31

Directions: Underline the simple subjects and put parentheses around the appositives. Punctuate correctly.

Example: <u>Arnold</u>, our class (president), gave an excellent speech.

1. Bob the musician gave a concert for our class.

2. Jim the leading actor in the school play broke his arm.

3. Sharon Murphy an architect received honorable mention for her design of the new library.

4. O. Henry a writer of short stories received worldwide acclaim.

5. Our dog a golden retriever loves people.

6. Joe's report a ten-page paper covered the topic thoroughly.

7. Carl's accomplishments a speed skater and a football linesman are truly an unusual combination.

8. Carl's brother a track star at Adams Junior High is also a good student.

9. The thick smoke a mixture of burnt rubber and fumes made her faint.

10. Mount Shasta a volcano towers thousands of feet above the surrounding valleys.

11. Miss Jones an excellent writer teaches writing in college.

12. Albert a born actor wants to major in drama.

13. Ed a computer expert plans to study computers this summer.

14. Sue a good soccer player leads the team in goals.

15. Al my brother is going to Alaska this summer.

16. Uncle Fred a mechanic always fixes my car.

17. Lassie a show dog earned huge salary for his owner.

18. Sam a dog trainer works for NBC.

19. Terry's typewriter an old Royal was finally discarded.

20. John my friend is moving to Chicago.

Direct Object

Some action verbs take objects. The **direct object** always answers the question *what?* or *whom?* The direct object is always a noun or pronoun.

> Jane found a surprise on her desk.
>
> | Jane | found | what? *surprise* |
> | *subject* | *verb* | *direct object* |
>
> James saw the movie three times.
>
> | James | saw | what? *movie* |
>
> Sally met her friend in San Diego.
>
> | Sally | met | whom? *friend* |

Exercise 32

Directions: Add direct objects to the following verbs. Be sure your object answers the question *what* or *whom.*

Example: We watched *the show.*

1. Joan saw _____

2. Shelly grabbed _____

3. Marvin took _____

4. The players won _____

5. The students chose _____

6. Winds caused _____

7. She tore _____

8. Andy washed _____

9. Marlene wrote _____

10. Sophia cut _____

11. Tim bought _____

12. We played _____

13. Jean gave _____

14. Our team saw _____

15. The baby had _____

16. Write _____

17. Rudy ate _____

18. I found _____

19. Cover _____

20. Paul earned _____

Exercise 33

Directions: Underline the subjects in the following paragraph. Put parentheses around the direct objects.

One morning Sally took a walk on the beach. For a while she watched the waves lapping at her feet. She searched for unusual sea shells. Suddenly a dog came toward her. Frightened, Sally saw a stick in the sand. She grabbed the stick and waved it in front of her. The dog stopped suddenly, turned, and went away. Sally breathed a sigh of relief. She ran and entered her house. She had enough excitement for one morning.

Exercise 34

Directions: If the verb has an object, write *O*. If the verb has no object, write *N*.

Example: opened door   *O*

_____	1. read newspaper	_____	14. cut pie
_____	2. published book	_____	15. learned lesson
_____	3. swirled near me	_____	16. walked slowly
_____	4. cast a shadow	_____	17. banged drum
_____	5. gave bracelet	_____	18. lost brother
_____	6. lowered the boom	_____	19. played ball
_____	7. shouted loudly	_____	20. ran quickly
_____	8. shouted instructions	_____	21. chose Jerry
_____	9. tasted apple	_____	22. pulled rope
_____	10. played in the park	_____	23. raised sails
_____	11. sold jewelry	_____	24. leaned sharply
_____	12. blamed sister	_____	25. learned quickly
_____	13. braced feet		

Compound Objects

Direct objects can also be compound.

I found apples and oranges in the basket.

Both *apples* and *oranges* are objects of the verb *found.*

She studied math, English, and Spanish during the summer months.

Math, English, and *Spanish* are objects of the verb *studied.*

Apposition to Direct Objects

Direct objects can have appositives.

> Last summer we visited Australia, a beautiful country.

In this sentence, *country* is in apposition to *Australia*. Both words are in the objective case.

Blair,	my best friend,	won several	awards	for his singing.
subject	*apposition*		*direct object*	

Jean,	a champion swimmer,	teaches	Kelly and Margie,
subject	*apposition*		*direct objects*

her little sisters,		at the YWCA every Saturday.
apposition to the direct objects.		

Exercise 35

Directions: Write *S* if the underlined word is a subject, *A* if it is an appositive, or *DO* if it is a direct object.

Example: Our <u>project</u>, a diorama, is due tomorrow.   *S*

_____ 1.   <u>Cathy Moore</u>, a math teacher, also coaches tennis.

_____ 2.   Jim, an excellent guitar player, will give a <u>concert</u> tomorrow.

_____ 3.   The girls in my class are taking Spanish, a popular <u>class</u>.

_____ 4.   The cheerleaders are having a banquet, the most important <u>event</u> of the year.

_____ 5.   My brother, a junior, wrote his history <u>paper</u> on George Washington.

_____ 6.   The student <u>council</u> made a unanimous decision.

_____ 7.   She found the <u>pen</u> in her bookbag.

_____ 8.   My <u>friends</u> worked at the zoo last summer.

_____ 9.   Did you send the <u>letter</u> yet?

_____ 10.   The actors, <u>students</u> from local high schools, took a bow.

Exercise 36

Directions: Underline the direct object and put parentheses around any appositives in the following sentences.

Example: Susan, an excellent (student), completed her final <u>paper</u> on time.

1. We always enjoy the class play and the spring concert, yearly programs at our school.

2. Carl, my cousin, won a tennis tournament on Friday.

3. Larry, an excellent artist and an outstanding athlete, will go to Stanford next year.

4. Nancy and Joyce had their first skiing lessons, a very unsettling experience.

5. After the game, the coach, a forceful individual, spoke angry words to his players.

6. George took a quart jar of pennies, the boys' contribution for the charities, to the principal's office.

7. During the rain storm, Janet, a six-year-old first grader, took her umbrella, skipped out the door, and splashed her way to the grocery store.

8. Laura Brown gave a heart-shaped locket, an heirloom from her own mother, to Mary, her only daughter, on her sixteenth birthday.

9. Julie, an average math student, suddenly remembered that her answer was wrong.

10. Last year my brother, a whiz on computers, earned a week's stay at the Hilton Hotel, a beautiful resort in Hawaii.

11. During the summer, Mike, a soccer player, received the highest mark on each test.

12. Dennis, our baseball coach, always has a winning team.

13. Tim, a slow runner, did not win the race.

14. We visited Yankee Stadium, a great experience.

15. We saw David Copperfield, an amazing magician.

16. My car, an old Chevrolet, was sold.

17. Did you see *Titanic*, a spectacular movie?

18. Michael Jordan, a multi-millionaire, has many sponsors.

19. Lisa's favorite pastime, skiing at Mammoth Mountain, gives her relaxation.

20. Richard, a graphic artist, works for a local newspaper.

21. Her computer, an IBM, does great work.

22. Lois Helvey, a geography teacher, has won several trophies.

23. Her hobby, making dolls, brings in a good income.

24. Kathy, a shy teenager, enjoys music.

25. His job, editing films, gives him access to many movies.

Exercise 37

Directions: On a separate piece of paper, write five original sentences using apposition to the subject and five sentences using apposition to the direct object.

Indirect Object

The **indirect object** of a verb names the person or thing to whom or for whom or for what the action was done. The sentence with an indirect object must also have a direct object. The *to* or *for* in the indirect object is always understood. The indirect object always precedes the direct object.

My mother gave my	brother	a dollar.
	to my brother	*direct object (what)*
My friend made	Tammy	a dress.
	for Tammy	*direct object (what)*

Exercise 38

Directions: Underline the indirect objects and put parentheses around the direct objects.

Example: She sent <u>Tom</u> a (letter).

1. The volunteers gave many people help.

2. The coach sent his players an important message.

3. Airports offer their controllers a challenge.

4. Joe sells his customers the paper.

5. The teacher offered Jerry advice.

6. His job gave Paul many challenges.

7. Mary made her mother a valentine.

8. Her brother sent Terry a necklace.

9. The principal offered the boys a reward.

10. Travel agents give their customers good service.

Exercise 39

Directions: Rewrite the following sentences, changing the *to* or *for* to indirect objects.

Example: Mrs. Jones made a costume for my brother.
           Mrs. Jones made my brother a costume.

1. Marion, the librarian, gave the book to Jim.

2. The police officer offered information to Carl.

3. The professor sent the report to Mario.

4. The teacher gave prizes to the winners.

5. Volunteers tell stories to the handicapped.

6. The teacher ordered special equipment for her class.

7. Jan Marie wrote a long letter to her mother.

8. The principal promised a free day to the students.

9. The teachers' guide gave ideas to the teachers.

10. Give an assignment to Melissa.

Note

Indirect objects can also have appositives.

Senator Jackson,	a brilliant individual,	wrote	Sally Jackson,
	apposition to subject		*indirect object*
a reporter,	a letter of apology.		
apposition to Sally	*direct object*		

Exercise 40

Directions: If the underlined noun is a subject, write *S*; if it is an indirect object, write *IO*; if it is a direct object, write *DO*.

Example: She gave <u>Jeff</u> the candy.   *IO*

_____ 1.   <u>Tammy,</u> my friend, will live in Canada next year.

_____ 2.   She sent her <u>father</u> her report card.

_____ 3.   Give the <u>boy</u> the money.

_____ 4.   Send <u>Julie</u> the package immediately.

_____ 5.   Brian gave the students excellent <u>advice</u>.

_____ 6.   Each <u>student</u> recited the poem by heart.

_____ 7.   The teacher chose <u>Jill</u> to lead the band.

_____ 8.   The volunteers offered the <u>poor</u> their services.

_____ 9.   The class sent <u>food</u> and <u>clothing</u> to the missions.

_____ 10. The <u>waves</u> pounded the pier.

_____ 11. Tom gave his <u>friends</u> a party.

_____ 12. The <u>answers</u> to the problems are in his book.

_____ 13. Give <u>Maria</u> the money.

_____ 14. He bought a <u>Volvo</u>.

_____ 15. My brother's <u>boat</u> won the race.

_____ 16. Leave the <u>bread</u> on the counter.

_____ 17. <u>Alice</u> studied hard for the math contest.

_____ 18. Dave's <u>house</u> was vandalized last night.

_____ 19. We watched the cross-country horse <u>race</u> last week.

_____ 20. The class gave their <u>teacher</u> a bouquet of flowers.

Possessive Nouns

Nouns in the possessive case show ownership. **Possessive nouns** use the apostrophe to show ownership.

the farm of my father	my father's farm
the habit of Jean	Jean's habit
the nest of the bird	the bird's nest

Rules to form possessive nouns

1. For nouns that do not end in *s*, add *'s*.

baby	baby's
boy	boy's
children	children's

2. For nouns that end in *s*, add an apostrophe ('). Names of persons that end in *s* form the plural by *'s*.

James	James's
dogs	dogs'
boys	boys'

Note

With **nouns**, the apostrophe indicates ownership.

Exercise 41

Directions: Change the following nouns to the possessive case.

Example: the folder of Chris *Chris' folder*

1. house of my uncle _____

2. toys of the children _____

3. problems of the plumber _____

4. feathers of the birds _____

5. fur of the cat _____

6. cage of the snake _____

7. trousers of the men _____

8. compensation of the workers _____

9. the hairdo of the lady _____

10. the engine of the car _____

11. the work of James _____

12. windows of the churches _____

13. rim of the glass _____

14. yoke of the oxen _____

15. bottle of the baby _____

16. idea of the coach _____

17. worry of the principal _____

18. hobbies of Patty _____

19. coat of the deer _____

20. retreat of the members _____

Exercise 42

Directions: Write singular possessive and plural possessive for the following nouns.

Example: dollar   *dollar's*   *dollars'*

   singular   possessive   plural possessive

1. student _____ _____

2. mouse _____ _____

3. brush _____ _____

4. hour _____ _____

5. soldier _____ _____

6. army   _____   _____

7. nickel   _____   _____

8. ball   _____   _____

9. day   _____   _____

10. examiner   _____   _____

11. child   _____   _____

12. country   _____   _____

13. villain   _____   _____

14. policeman   _____   _____

15. match   _____   _____

16. curtain   _____   _____

17. lady   _____   _____

18. chicken   _____   _____

19. officer   _____   _____

20. nurse   _____   _____

Exercise 43

Directions: On another piece of paper, write five sentences using singular possessives and five sentences using plural possessives.

Unit 2 Review

1. A noun is the name of a person, place, thing, or idea.

2. There are different kinds of nouns: proper nouns, common nouns, and abstract nouns. Proper nouns refer to a specific person, place, thing, or idea, and must be capitalized. Common nouns refer to any person, place, thing, or idea, and are not capitalized. Abstract nouns have a quality or idea, and are not capitalized.

3. Nouns are singular or plural. A singular noun names only one person, place, thing, or idea. A plural noun names more than one.

4. The gender of nouns is either masculine, feminine, or neuter.

5. Nouns have different uses in a sentence.

   a. Nouns are used as the subject of a sentence. Noun subjects can also have apposition.

   b. Nouns are used as the direct object of a verb. They answer the questions *what?* or *whom?* Direct objects can have appositives.

   c. Nouns are used as the indirect object. They can name the person or thing *to* or *for* the action was done. An indirect object must always have a direct object.

   d. Nouns are used to show possession. The apostrophe is used with nouns to indicate ownership. When the noun does not end in *s,* add *'s.* When a plural ends in *s,* add an apostrophe.

Unit 2
Review Test

Part A.

Directions: If the sentence is capitalized correctly, write *C.* If it is capitalized incorrectly, write *I.*

_____ 1. My father insists on visiting the south this summer.

_____ 2. Have you ever visited the Huntington Library?

_____ 3. One summer we sailed down the Mississippi river.

_____ 4. My friend lives in the San Fernando Valley.

_____ 5. Jenny attends the Riverhead High School.

_____ 6. We went to the Metropolitan Museum of Art last year.

_____ 7. Bob belongs to the Democratic Party.

_____ 8. The school is always closed on Labor Day.

_____ 9. The Red Cross helps people in distress.

_____ 10. The best season for me is Spring.

Part B.

Directions: Underline the simple subject and put parentheses around any appositives. Punctuate correctly.

1. His favorite chair a recliner gets lots of use.

2. The literature of America began in Colonial days.

3. Abigail Adams the wife of John Quincy Adams is noted for her letters.

4. A swarm of bees can be hazardous.

5. A pack of dogs ran through the mall.

6. A flock of geese settled in my back yard.

7. Benjamin Franklin a genius wrote a popular autobiography.

8. Tom an eighth grader takes pictures of school activities.

9. His latest book a mystery novel is popular with mystery lovers.

10. Students in her class love to debate.

Directions: Underline the direct objects and put parentheses around the indirect objects.

1. Please give Joe his papers.

2. Carol made her teacher a bookcase.

3. Coach Mack taught his team many valuable plays.

4. Give the team a rousing welcome.

5. My mother bought Jack and Bill their plane tickets to Hawaii.

6. The postman brought Terry a letter.

7. Jean my sister made Jim and Pete a terrific lunch.

8. The police officer brought Tom the sad news.

9. The guide gave our class special attention.

10. My uncle gave the twins a ride to the airport.

Directions: Make the following underlined nouns possessive.

1. We found <u>Jerry</u> pencil in his desk. _____

2. They have many <u>children</u> games. _____

3. Those <u>babies</u> blankets are too expensive. _____

4. The <u>coaches</u> suggestions are always important. _____

5. We don't mind a <u>days</u> journey. _____

6. My <u>grandmother</u> house needs paint. _____

7. The <u>church</u> stained-glass windows are beautiful. _____

8. The elderly <u>woman</u> wheelchair broke in an accident. _____

9. The <u>oxen</u> yoke was heavy. _____

10. The <u>principal</u> talk was to the point. _____

Directions: If the verb has an object, write *O*. If the verb has no object, write *N*.

_____ 1. went to the fair

_____ 2. cooked dinner

_____ 3. guessed correctly

_____ 4. planned a diet

_____ 5. joined the army

_____ 6. left for Europe

_____ 7. lost his way

_____ 8. played soccer

_____ 9. watched the game

_____ 10. have a headache

Directions: Combine the following sentences using appositives. Punctuate correctly.

1. Larry had a serious fall. He is an eighth grade student.

2. Mary will graduate in June. She is an honor student.

3. Leo might lose his job. He is a teacher of woodworking.

4. Bob collects postage stamps. It is a money-making pastime.

5. Mosquitoes are carriers of diseases. They thrive in warm water.

6. The tree was cut down. It was a beautiful pine tree.

7. Barb received a pay increase. She is a diligent worker.

8. Terry received a scholarship to Pepperdine University. She is an art major.

9. Mr. Goldman is a short gentleman. He is a conscientious tailor.

10. The swampy Everglades has many alligators. The Everglades is Florida's treasure.

What Is a Verb?

A **verb** is the simple predicate of a sentence. It generally shows action as well as time (tense) and tells what the subject is, was, or will be doing. It may also show what is, was, or will be done to the subject. Every sentence must have a verb.

> John hit the ball over the fence.

John is the subject. The verb *hit* tells what the subject is doing.

> The ball was hit.

Ball is the subject. The verb *was hit* tells what was done to the subject. This kind of verb will be studied later.

> Maria sings in the choir.

Maria is the subject. The verb *sings* tells what Maria does.

Exercise 44

Directions: Underline the simple subjects and put parentheses around the simple predicates in the following sentences.

Example: <u>Joe</u> *(runs)* five miles and *(lifts)* weights for an hour.

1. The conductor took our tickets.

2. The swimmer won a gold medal for the 500-meter race.

3. The crowd of spectators showed approval by clapping.

4. The general in the army issued an order to his lieutenant.

5. Jenny rises early and eats breakfast with her teammates.

6. Michelle rode her favorite horse all morning.

7. The tray of food intensified everyone's appetite.

8. The official canceled the game.

9. Terry dashed across the finish line and won the trophy.

10. Kate and Jim carted the books to the library and received a reward.

11. Carl entered the room, turned on the light, and sank into a chair.

12. The bottle of cranberry juice spilled in the refrigerator.

13. The Egyptians needed a time system.

14. Sun causes cancer of the skin for many people.

15. Carmen saw Todd in the distance.

16. My mother prepares excellent meals.

17. Their bottles of wine sold very reasonably.

18. A number of members from another club joined us.

19. Choose your friends carefully.

20. Grandma waters her garden every morning.

Exercise 45

Directions: If the sentences in **Exercise 44** have verbs that ask *what* or *whom*, circle the verb and its object. If there is no direct object, label the sentence *No*.

Example: Joe (runs) five (miles) and (lifts) (weights) for an hour.

Exercise 46

Directions: Add appropriate verbs to make your own sentences.

Example: Bob *raced* down the track.

1. Carol _____ her algebra every evening.

2. The injured man _____ up the steps.

3. The freight train _____ down the tracks.

4. Caroline _____ that movie before.

5. The rain _____ the crops.

6. Jane _____ the paper into two parts.

7. Keith _____ mystery stories.

8. Tim _____ about his trip to India.

9. Her brother _____ baseball cards.

10. Her horse _____ the race.

State-of-Being Verbs

Some verbs have no action. They are **state-of-being verbs**: *am, is, was, were, be, been.*

A subject cannot *am* or *is*, for example. No action is involved with state-of-being verbs. They are also called linking verbs because they often link the subject with a word in the predicate.

Pete is captain of the soccer team.

The subject is *Pete*. Pete is not acting. The verb *is* links *Pete* to *captain*. Pete and captain are the same person.

May has been captain of the softball team for two years.

May and *captain* are the same. Captain tells what May has been.

Don was chairman of the committee.

Don is the subject. *Was* links Don to chairman.

Alisha will be a cheerleader next year.

Alisha is the subject. *Will be* links Alisha to cheerleader.

Exercise 47

Directions: Underline the state-of-being verbs in the following sentences. On the blank, write the word that is linked to the subject.

Example: Dr. Kind <u>is</u> Bob's favorite doctor.   *doctor*

1. Barbara is an excellent swimmer. _____

2. Rudy has been the coach for five years. _____

3. Zinc is an important mineral. _____

4. The students were all leaders. _____

5. She will be class treasurer next year. _____

6. I am president of our class. _____

7. Sandra was a student at UCSB. _____

8. Mark was the best player. _____

9. The moon was the calendar for ancient tribes. _____

10. Astronaut Neil Armstrong was the first man on the moon. _____

Exercise 48

Directions: If the verb is linking, write *L*; if it is not linking, write *N*. Remember, if the verb is linking, the subject is not acting.

Example: Fred will be a freshman next year.   *L*

_____ 1.   Marcos was a good baseball player.

_____ 2.   Sara hit the ball for a home run.

_____ 3.   She was working for her uncle.

_____ 4.   She was a good worker.

_____ 5.   Elena will be a writer some day.

_____ 6. Pablo enjoys painting pictures.

_____ 7. Maria is an excellent cook.

_____ 8. Irene put the book on the shelf.

_____ 9. Paul earned a scholarship for high school.

_____ 10. Anna will be an excellent secretary someday.

_____ 11. My mother is a great singer.

_____ 12. Alice chose Jack for her partner.

_____ 13. Sara is a good student.

_____ 14. Laura has been an architect for three months.

_____ 15. Rebecca skates brilliantly.

_____ 16. Mr. Henderson will retire next month.

_____ 17. Fred loves tomato soup.

_____ 18. Carlos will be the next world champion fighter.

_____ 19. Thomas brought several books to class.

_____ 20. Teresa is an excellent actress.

Exercise 49

Directions: Write the subject, the linking verb, and what it links.

Example: Teresa was the lead in the play.   *Teresa was lead*

1. Irene and Celia were both chairpersons.

2. Ricardo was a clever magician.

3. Jaime should be the lead in the play.

4. He is also a good dancer.

5. Fred was a skater.

6. Pablo has been captain for two years.

7. He will be manager next year.

8. Becky is an actress.

9. David was an inventor.

10. Bob was an accountant.

Exercise 50

Directions: If the verb is linking, underline it and write *L*. If it is an action verb, write *A*. Remember, when nouns follow state-of-being verbs, the verbs are linking.

Example: has been principal   *L*

_____ 1. is chairperson

_____ 2. were fighting

_____ 3. has been general

_____ 4. were taken

_____ 5. am secretary

_____ 6. were stolen

_____ 7. were champions

_____ 8. will be skiing

_____ 9. had been lieutenant

_____ 10. should be writer

_____ 11. will be manager

_____ 12. has been skating

_____ 13. had been enjoying

_____ 14. were players

_____ 15. was scientist

_____ 16. were running

_____ 17. will be going

_____ 18. will be librarian

_____ 19. had been ruined

_____ 20. should be student

Exercise 51

Directions: Underline all verbs. Put parentheses around the direct objects and circle the word that completes a linking verb.

Example: Debbie <u>took</u> her little *(sister)* to the show.

1. Michelle sent her brother a pen.

2. The tragedy caused pain.

3. The librarian was a bookworm.

4. Jean is a seamstress.

5. Gloria will graduate in June.

6. Sam takes his work seriously.

7. She trusted Jerry.

8. Our coach is a great swimmer.

9. They painted their boat.

10. I have written several plays.

11. Life is not a rose garden.

12. The accident totaled his car.

13. The car was a Taurus.

14. Pete sings in the choir.

15. Sue understands computers.

16. Our teacher is a good speaker.

17. I bought several mystery novels.

18. Everyone felt drops of rain.

19. Joe was a cartoonist.

20. Tom Cruise is a great actor.

Principal Parts of Verbs

Every verb has three principal parts. They build the six tenses.

1. *Regular verbs*

    Regular verbs have the same past tense and past participle. Add *ed* to the present tense: joke, joked, joked.

2. *Irregular verbs*

    Irregular verbs form their past tense and past participle in different ways.

    a. by keeping the same form for the past and past participle:

bring	brought	brought
send	sent	sent

    b. by changing all forms:

ring	rang	rung
go	went	gone

    c. by making no change:

cut	cut	cut
hurt	hurt	hurt

    It is wise to memorize the principal parts of difficult irregular verbs that are used frequently. Remember, you must add *have* or *has* with the past participle. The past participle by itself is not a verb. It must have *have, has,* or *had* to make it a verb.

Frequently Used Irregular Verbs

have	has	had
begin	began	begun
blow	blew	blown
break	broke	broken
choose	chose	chosen
come	came	come
do	did	done
eat	ate	eaten
fall	fell	fallen
go	went	gone
freeze	froze	frozen
rise	rose	risen
run	run	run
see	saw	seen
shrink	shrank	shrunk
sit	sat	sat
set	set	set
speak	spoke	spoken
steal	stole	stolen
take	took	taken
write	wrote	written

Exercise 52

Directions: Complete the following sentences with the correct form of the verb.

Example: call   She had *called* me twice.

1. give   She has _____ that speech before.

2. see   They had_____ that movie last week.

3. go   She will _____ with us tomorrow.

4. drive   Joe _____ very carelessly.

5. drink   Julie_____ the milk in one gulp.

6. know   Jody_____ the lesson well.

7. take   Bill has always_____ an interest in books.

8. ring   The principal had already _____ the bell.

9. fall   Myra _____ down the steps last night.

10. freeze   He always _____ the fish.

11. write   Will you _____ the next report?

12. throw   In anger, he _____ the ball.

13. ride   Have you ever _____ with him?

14. blow   The storm has _____ down the tree.

15. burst   The balloon had _____ on impact.

16. swim   Ted _____ each morning.

17. begin   We _____ the long walk home.

18. wear   Susie has _____ that sweater all year.

19. eat   Jane had _____ there before.

20. come   My nephew _____ for my graduation.

21. shrink   Her clothes have _____ .

22. show   Carol _____ her picture to the class.

23. sink   The boat _____ quickly.

24. cut   Do not _____ the pattern on that table.

25. swim   She has _____ there all last summer.

Verb Tenses

Verbs have six tenses: present, past, future, present perfect, past perfect, and future perfect.

1. *Present tense*—action going on or a continuing recurring action

> Sally plays the violin.
>
> Joe eats in the cafeteria.
>
> Irene sings in the choir.
>
> The bus departs daily from the school grounds.

To form the third person singular, add *s*.

> writes   sings
>
> plays   works
>
> gives

2. *Past tense*—action is completed

> Our team won the game.
>
> They played in the park.
>
> Irene sang in the choir yesterday.

3. *Future tense*—action that is going to happen

> Bob will write a letter to his mother.
>
> Jill will return the book to the library.
>
> He will ride his bike to school.

4. *Present Perfect*—uses the auxiliary verbs *have* and *has*; action continuing in the present

> She has slept all afternoon.
>
> Barbara has worked there for two years.

5. *Past Perfect*—uses the auxiliary verb *had*

6. *Future Perfect*—not used very frequently

The most important tenses in your writing are present, past, and future. The other tenses will be stressed in high school.

Be aware that the third principal part is not a verb; you must use *have, has,* or *had.* In writing, be consistent in your use of tenses.

Directions: Underline each verb and write its tense.

Example: We <u>had</u> <u>been</u> <u>scheduled</u> for a meeting. *past perfect*

1. Jerry plans his work schedule every day. _____

2. He planted his roses a little early this year. _____

3. Francis will play soccer next year. _____

4. Carol sings in the choir every Sunday. _____

5. Mark will move to Idaho this summer. _____

6. She has taken the packages to the post office. _____

7. She turned the key in the lock. _____

8. Juan studies Spanish every Saturday morning. _____

9. James will become an engineer. _____

10. The class will collect money for the poor. _____

11. Greg noticed his error right away. _____

12. My first ball sank into the pond. _____

13. Fred had already given me the money. _____

14. Andrea usually studies by herself. _____

15. Isabel will take ballet. _____

16. He had done that work before. _____

17. Jose will join the Marines. _____

18. We held a celebration for our victory. _____

19. We chose the right candidate. _____

20. I will do my project tomorrow. _____

Tense of the State-of-Being Verbs

Present Tense: am, is, are

Past Tense: was, were

Future Tense: will be

Present Perfect: has been, have been

Past Perfect: had been

Future Perfect: will have been

Exercise 54

Directions: Underline the verb in each sentence. Give the tense of the verb and put parentheses around the word it links to the subject.

Example: The deadline <u>was</u> last (Tuesday).   *past*

1.   Bob was a good tennis player.   _____

2.   Joe has been captain for three years.   _____

3.   Maria will be a great secretary.   _____

4.   Teresa is a graceful ice skater.   _____

5.   Jaime was the best player on the team.   _____

6.   He has also been the captain.   _____

7.   My cousin had been an actress.   _____

8.   They are winners in the math contest.   _____

9.   All of the contestants were drama students. _____

10. Bob is a trombone player in the band.   _____

Progressive Form of Verbs

Progressive verbs show continuous action. They are used with state-of-being verbs that indicate the tense.

> She was working with her aunt.
>
> He is trying hard.

Add *ing* to the present tense of a verb to get the progressive form.

write	writing
give	giving
send	sending

Directions: Underline the progressive verb and give its tense.

Example: The baby <u>is</u> <u>crying.</u>   *present progressive*

1. Jon is playing in the band.   _____

2. Julie has been working there for years.   _____

3. Bert is playing football.   _____

4. Thelma will be running track this year.   _____

5. They were suing the company.   _____

6. My father is going to Paris.   _____

7. The flowers were blooming.   _____

8. Our team was winning the contest.   _____

9. James is giving a talk next week.   _____

10. Gloria will be leaving tomorrow.   _____

11. The class is studying algebra.   _____

12. The children were skating at the rink.   _____

13. Jill is going to the mall.   _____

14. She is watching television.   _____

15. Maria was skiing in Mammoth.   _____

16. My friend will be leaving for Canada.   _____

17. Brian was enjoying the play.   _____

18. Laura will be singing professionally.   _____

19. Sue will be writing her essay tonight.   _____

20. Pete was sleeping on the job.   _____

Active and Passive Voice

Active Voice

A verb is in the **active voice** when the subject performs the action of the verb.

> Jerry paints many pictures.

Jerry is the subject. He is acting. The verb is in the active voice.

> Miguel will travel to Japan this summer.

Miguel is the subject. The verb *will travel* is what he will do. The verb is in the active voice.

Passive Voice

A verb is in the **passive voice** when the subject receives the action. The direct object in an active voice sentence becomes the subject of a passive voice sentence.

> The backpack was taken to school by Maria.

The backpack is the subject (receiver of the action), followed by a passive voice verb and the object of a preposition.

> Maria took her backpack to school.

Maria is the subject (doer of the action). The verb *took* is in the active voice. *Backpack* (the direct object) receives the action.

> The book   was found   by John.
> *Receiver*   *passive voice verb*   *object of a preposition*

> John   found   the book.
> *Doer*   *active voice verb*   *direct object*

Often in using passive voice the subject doer is lost or it becomes the object of the preposition *by.*

> Sally wrote a letter.
>
> John finished the homework.

In both of these sentences, the subject is the doer of the action.

> A letter was written by Sally.
>
> The homework was finished by John.

In both of these sentences, the subject is the receiver of the action.

Only verbs with objects can be changed into passive voice because the object, or receiver of the action, becomes the subject. Action verbs with no receiver are always active voice.

> Carol   hit   the ball.
> *Subject doer*   *active voice*   *receiver*

> The ball   was hit   by Carol.
> *Subject receiver*   *passive voice*   *object of preposition*

> Richard   plays   soccer.
> *Subject doer*   *active voice verb*   *receiver*

> Soccer   is played   by Richard.
> *Subject receiver*   *object of preposition*

Directions: Write *D* if the subject is the doer and *R* if it is the receiver.

Example: Lisa ate   *D*

_____ 1. John went

_____ 2. Lois called

_____ 3. Room was painted

_____ 4. Car was sold

_____ 5. The club planned

_____ 6. Rain destroyed

_____ 7. River overflowed

_____ 8. Picture was taken

_____ 9. Joe sent

_____ 10. The dog raced

_____ 11. Store was closed

_____ 12. Sally made

_____ 13. Play has been seen

_____ 14. He took

_____ 15. Jerry rode

_____ 16. Office closed

_____ 17. Subpoena was served

_____ 18. Rain flooded

_____ 19. Prizes were awarded

_____ 20. Clothes were given

Directions: If the subject is the doer, write *D*; if the subject is the receiver, write *R*.

Example: The tests were graded by the teacher. *R*

_____ 1.   The desks were varnished during the summer.

_____ 2.   Laura put her answer on the board.

_____ 3.   Sue answered the question correctly.

_____ 4.   The books were printed by the American Book Company.

_____ 5.   The speech was given by Tom.

_____ 6.   Those books must be returned to the library.

_____ 7.   The eighth grade will plan the dance.

_____ 8.   The party will be given by my mother.

_____ 9.   The papers were distributed to the class.

_____ 10. The mail has been taken to the mailbox.

_____ 11. The classroom doors are locked at 5:00 P.M.

_____ 12. The mural was painted by the art class.

_____ 13. The honors were awarded at the Friday assembly.

_____ 14. The rooms will be painted during vacation.

_____ 15. Pat scoured the neighborhood for work.

_____ 16. The homeless man begged for some food.

_____ 17. The kitchen was refinished after the earthquake.

_____ 18. The sound of the alarm scared us all.

_____ 19. The computer was fixed immediately.

_____ 20. Professor Goldman wrote a letter of complaint.

Using Passive Voice

Sentences are either **active** or **passive voice**. Using active voice makes your writing more forceful because active verbs stress action. Passive voice is used when the subject is not known or not important. Passive voice often weakens writing, so use it sparingly.

> Tom was injured in an accident. (Doer not known)
>
> The goods were shipped last week. (Doer unimportant)

In passive voice, the state-of-being verb determines the tense.

> The dishes were washed. (past tense)
>
> The returns will be forwarded to you. (future tense)

Exercise 58

Directions: Underline the verbs in the following sentences. Then change the passive voice verbs to active voice. If there is no doer, add one.

Example: The books <u>were packed</u> in boxes.   *Boys packed the books in boxes.*

1. The novel was read by the entire class. _____

2. The costume was chosen by my sister. _____

3. The picture was painted by Jean. _____

4. The video was shown to the team. _____

5. The speech will be given later. _____

6. His hair was trimmed. _____

7. The room will be painted by Barbara. _____

8. Her clothes were washed last night. _____

9. The room was cleaned. _____

10. The musical was enjoyed by everyone. _____

Exercise 59

Directions: Underline the verb. Write *A* if the verb is in the active voice or *P* if it is in the passive voice.

Example: The car <u>was washed</u> yesterday.   *P*

_____ 1. Roberto has eaten dinner.

_____ 2. Jason likes ice cream.

_____ 3. The team practiced wrestling after school.

_____ 4. Connie typed the letter.

_____ 5. Our car was taken to the machine shop.

_____ 6. The muffler was fixed.

_____ 7. The headlight on the car was broken.

_____ 8. That story had been told before.

_____ 9. Gene broke his arm while playing soccer.

_____ 10. All the tables were refinished.

_____ 11. Connie knitted a shawl for a Christmas present.

_____ 12. A doll house was designed by my father.

_____ 13. Paul enjoys the computer.

_____ 14. The grass will be mowed by my brother.

_____ 15. My little sister made her bed.

_____ 16. All the dishes were washed by my father.

_____ 17. We played games on the computer all evening.

_____ 18. Our cellar was flooded by a storm.

_____ 19. My mother has grown potatoes before.

_____ 20. The weeds were uprooted.

Exercise 60

Directions: Change the active-voice verbs in **Exercise 59** to passive voice. Change the passive verbs to active voice. If no doer is given, add one.

Example: The car was washed yesterday. *We washed the car yesterday.*

Exercise 61

Directions: Write a paragraph about an experience you had. Use only active-voice verbs. Underline your verbs.

Note
Not or *never* is not a part of a verb phrase.

>   We had not finished our project.   *Had finished* is the verb.

Review
Passive voice has the third principal part of the verb following the state-of-being verb.

>   had been prepared   has been reviewed   were written

Linking verbs have a noun following the state-of-being verb.

>   is president   will be manager   were partners

Progressive verbs have verbs with *ing* following state-of-being verbs.

>   will be walking   were enjoying   is taking

Exercise 62

Part A.

Directions: Change passive voice verbs to active voice. If no doer is given, add one. Do not change tense.

Example: The books were bought during the summer. *We bought the books during the summer.*

1. Cheers were led by the cheerleaders.

2. The concert was enjoyed by everyone.

3. The documents will be sealed by the judge.

4. The store was swept.

5. The play was enjoyed by our class.

6. The players were challenged by the captain.

7. The curtains had been purchased by the drama coach.

8. The office will be remodeled by the booster club.

9. The hiker was saved by the firemen.

10. The clubhouse has been cleaned.

Part B.

Directions: Change the verbs to the progressive form. Do not change tense.

Example: Terry threw her papers on the desk. *Terry was throwing her papers on the desk.*

1. Fred will learn computers this summer.

2. The birds flew over the school.

3. Sara brushes her teeth.

4. Bob ate the peanuts.

5. The girls threw the ball.

6. We moved yesterday.

7. Our dog runs to the water.

8. We play volleyball in our backyard.

9. Al works at Taco Bell.

10. They chose a mascot.

Subject-Verb Agreement

The subject and verb must always agree in number. If the subject is singular, the verb is singular; if the subject is plural, the verb is plural.

Most verbs ending in *s* are singular.

> The box has a red label.

Box is singular, so the verb is singular.

> The boxes have red labels.

Boxes is plural, so the verb is plural.

singular	plural
I give	we give
you give	you give
he, she, it gives	they give

a. Add *s* to verbs with third person singular subjects.

write	writes
find	finds
give	gives
Susan writes well.	(she writes)
Keith likes baseball.	(he likes)

b. Add *es* to verbs ending in *ch, s, sh, x,* or *z.*

> watch   watches
>
> fix   fixes
>
> Al fixes anything that is broken.

c. Change the *y* to *i* and add *es* to verbs ending in a consonant and *y,* singular.

> carry   carries
>
> fly   flies
>
> hurry   hurries
>
> Jane hurries home from school each afternoon.

d. Add *es* to verbs ending in *o.*

> do   does
>
> go   goes
>
> Bill does his homework faithfully.

Exercise 63

Directions: Change the following verbs to third person singular.

Example: find *finds*

1. inform   _____

2. catch   _____

3. carry   _____

4. ride   _____

5. reply   _____

6. veto   _____

7. buzz   _____

8. employ   _____

9. try   _____

10. repair   _____

11. buy   _____

12. watch   _____

13. pass   _____

14. run   _____

15. mix   _____

16. crush _____

17. laugh _____

18. race _____

19. sit _____

20. echo _____

Directions: Write the present tense form of the verb.

Example: My brother (like) *likes* to play tennis.

1. John (grow) _____ tomatoes in his garden.

2. He (amplify) _____ the message.

3. The car (pitch) _____ from side to side.

4. Jon (make) _____ repairs on his car.

5. Lois (handle) _____ that material with care.

6. Luis (open) _____ the gate each morning.

7. Lightning (fill) _____ the sky.

8. The prisoner (go) _____ quietly

9. Marilyn (take) _____ the bus each morning.

10. The teacher (see) _____ the mistakes.

11. Joe (write) _____ regularly to his mom.

12. Maria (find) _____ my class rather boring.

13. Jeanine (show) _____ her authority when possible.

14. Brian (throw) _____ the baseball every morning.

15. Gladys (enjoy) _____ her garden of roses.

16. Tim (tear) _____ his papers in two.

17. Joanie (eat) _____ with her father each Sunday.

18. Ned (brag) _____ about his athletic ability.

19. My sister (know) _____ when to keep silent.

20. Mark (believe) _____ in his future.

The simple subject always controls the verb.

      A bundle of papers was dumped on our lawn.

The subject is *bundle*, not *papers*. The verb is singular.

Exercise 65

Directions: Underline the subjects of the following sentences and write the correct form of the verb.

Example: The <u>group</u> of friends (meet) *meets* once a week.

1. A truck of tomatoes (pass) _____ our house frequently.

2. My sister with her friends (like) _____ to go swimming.

3. A dish of peaches (sit) _____ on the table.

4. A barrel of pickles (stand) _____ in the back of the store.

5. A pot of potatoes (boil) _____ on the stove.

6. The doctor with his assistants (give) _____ hours of service to the poor.

7. Professor Jensen with Professor Harrison (visit) _____ the Medical Center once a week.

8. A shelf of books (break) _____ from the wall.

9. A sliver of glass (cut) _____ his arm.

10. A bundle of papers (burn) _____ quickly.

Agreement with Compound Subjects.

a. Subjects joined by *and* usually take a plural verb whether the subjects are singular or plural.

      Winds and rain cause much damage.

b. Singular subjects joined by *or* or *nor* take a singular verb. Plural subjects take a plural verb.

c. The noun nearest to the *or* or *nor* controls the verb.

      Dave or Bill wins the championship.   (Bill wins)

      Apples or oranges were on sale.   (oranges were)

Jean or her parents are going to the meeting.   (parents are)

Her parents or Jean is going to the meeting.   (Jean is)

Exercise 66

Directions: Complete the sentences with the correct form of the verb. Keep your verbs in the present tense.

Example: turn   Jenny *turns* on the light.

1. write   Lois and her sister _____ letters frequently.

2. enjoy   Tom or his parents _____ skiing.

3. speak   The victims or their attorney _____ to the parents about the crime.

4. want   The senator or the representatives _____ to hold a meeting immediately.

5. is, are   A loan or a scholarship _____ available for students with good marks.

6. go   A desk or a bed _____ into that room.

7. plan   The coach or the team members _____ to go on a trip to Maine.

8. is, are   The girls or their coach _____ arranging a trip to the mountains.

9. is, are   A boat or a car _____ on display at the new store.

10. do   Mary or her friends _____ many things together.

11. shoot   He _____ baskets every evening.

12. give   Kevin _____ his friend some of his lunch.

13. show   Sam _____ off his new car.

14. write   My sister in college _____ my mom every week.

15. is, are   The flowers or the plants _____ beautiful.

16. save   A computer or a typewriter _____ time.

17. share   My uncle _____ his boat with me.

18. ride   Jim _____ his bike to school each morning.

19. send   Joe or Jean _____ him greetings.

20. see   My teacher _____ every mistake.

21. believe   We _____ in freedom.

22. use   Joe _____ his time well.

23. play   I _____ on the basketball court every day.

24. throw   She _____ a fast softball.

25. buy   Mary always _____ the groceries for her mother.

26. bring   Julie _____ an apple to school each day.

27. wear   Jim _____ old shoes to school.

28. find   Jeff often _____ notes in his desk.

29. keep   Terry _____ a journal of her trips.

30. lose   Tim often _____ his homework.

1. A verb is the simple predicate of a sentence. It frequently shows action and tells what the subject is, was, or will be doing or what is, was, or will be done to the subject.

2. State-of-being verbs are *am, is, are, was, were, be,* and *been.* They have no action. State-of-being verbs are also called linking verbs because they often link the subject with a word in the predicate.

3. Verbs have three principal parts that build the six tenses.

   a. The three principal parts are present, past, and past participle.

      It is wise to memorize the principal parts of the most difficult irregular verbs.

      Add the auxiliary verbs *have, has,* and *had* to the past participle to make it a verb. By itself, the past participle is not a verb.

   b. The six tenses are present, past, future, present perfect, past perfect, and future perfect. The perfect tenses will be studied in detail in high school. The present, past and future tenses should be learned thoroughly and used consistently.

      Memorize the tense of the state-of-being verbs.

Present:	am, is, are
Past:	was, were
Future:	will be
Present perfect:	have, has been
Past perfect:	had been
Future perfect:	will have been

4. Verbs have progressive forms that show continuous action. They are used with state-of-being verbs that indicate the tense. To make a progressive verb, add *ing* to the present tense.

5. Verbs have voice: active and passive. The verb speaks actively when the subject is the doer. It speaks passively when the subject is the receiver.

6. a. Passive voice: the third principal part of the verb follows a state-of-being verb.

   b. Linking verbs: a noun follows state-of-being verb.

   c. Progressive form: add *ing* to a present tense verb preceded by a state-of-being verb.

7. Verbs must always agree in number with the noun subject. A singular subject takes a singular verb. A plural subject takes a plural verb. Subjects joined by *and* usually take a plural verb.

Unit 3
Review Test

Part A.

Directions: Give the tense of the following verbs.

1. had given _____
2. were _____
3. has sent _____
4. is _____
5. was _____
6. will go _____
7. have conquered _____
8. had worn _____
9. will write _____
10. have seen _____
11. had broken _____
12. has promised _____
13. practiced _____
14. is reviewing _____
15. has washed _____
16. were deciding _____
17. gives _____
18. has been watching _____
19. begins _____
20. enjoyed _____

Part B.

Directions: Label the following verbs *A* for active voice or *P* for passive voice.

_____ 1. will be allowed   _____ 8. ate

_____ 2. swallowed   _____ 9. will enter

_____ 3. begins   _____ 10. stored

_____ 4. are forgotten   _____ 11. has been plowed

_____ 5. has eaten   _____ 12. will look

_____ 6. were chosen   _____ 13. pushed

_____ 7. have batted   _____ 14. had been painted

_____ 15. will remove   _____ 18. will clean

_____ 16. has prepared   _____ 19. operates

_____ 17. have been removed   _____ 20. has been mixed

Part C.

Directions: Underline the verbs in the following sentences. Then mark *PA* for passive, *PR* for progressive, or *L* for linking.

_____ 1. Pete is enjoying his ride in the country.

_____ 2. She has been a typist for twenty years.

_____ 3. That jewelry has been stolen.

_____ 4. The thief was captured.

_____ 5. Marvin has been working there for five years.

_____ 6. They are walking to town.

_____ 7. She is an accountant.

_____ 8. Jerry will be leaving soon.

_____ 9. Oil was mixed with the vinegar.

_____ 10. The words have been mispronounced.

_____ 11. The book is a masterpiece.

_____ 12. She will be the next winner.

_____ 13. James was skiing all weekend.

_____ 14. He is a champion skier.

_____ 15. The fire will be covered with dirt.

_____ 16. Are you eating in the cafeteria?

_____ 17. Brian has been playing football for two years.

_____ 18. He is a quarterback on the team.

_____ 19. John has been an Eagle scout since last year.

_____ 20. My project is finally completed.

Part D.

Directions: Write the correct verb form for third person singular.

1. send (past perfect) _____

2. go (past) _____

3. finished (present perfect) _____

4. see (present progressive) _____

5. wear (future) _____

6. throw (past) _____

7. teach (future) _____

8. keep (present perfect) _____

9. lock (past progressive) _____

10. clean (future) _____

11. begin (past) _____

12. pay (future) _____

13. cover (present perfect) _____

14. decide (past perfect) _____

15. rise (past) _____

Directions: Complete the following sentences with the correct present tense of each verb.

1. She (rely) _____ on his judgment.

2. He (play) _____ in the park after school.

3. Peggy (trust) _____ Bob.

4. Mary (portray) _____ characters from her plays.

5. My car (do) _____ run very well.

6. Carlos and Louise (plan) _____ to go on a trip.

7. My computer (need) _____ to be fixed.

8. Linda (begin) _____ her vacation today.

9. We (practice) _____ every morning.

10. Thieves (steal) _____ very easily.

11. Mary or her sister (want) _____ to go to the concert.

12. Jean or her friends (take) _____ Spanish.

13. The players or the coach (lift) _____ weights.

14. Jane (wish) _____ to go home early.

15. The principal (ring) _____ the bell for dismissal.

16. The students (try) _____ hard each day.

17. The rain (make) _____ queer noises in my house.

18. Jon and his cousin (repair) _____ cars for a living.

19. The whistle (blow) _____ each night.

20. They (find) _____ the class boring.

21. Jean or her sister (write) _____ well.

22. Brian or his cousins (fly) _____ airplanes.

23. The professor often (speak) _____ quietly.

24. He always (leave) _____ at noon.

25. Joe and Pete (jog) _____ every morning.

Unit 4
Pronouns

What Is a Pronoun?

A **pronoun** is a word that takes the place of a noun or refers to a noun. *Pro* means "for." A pronoun, therefore, is a word that is used for a noun.

Ted took his bike to the mechanic to be fixed.

The pronoun *his* refers to *Ted*.

Bob and Paul ate their lunches in the cafeteria.

Their is a pronoun that refers to *Bob and Paul*.

Antecedents

Antecedents are the noun or nouns to which a pronoun refers.

Our team won its first championship.

In this sentence the antecedent for *its* is *team*.

Sue saw her article in the newspaper.

Sue is the antecedent for the pronoun *her*.

Note

Antecedents can also come after the pronoun.

Pronouns generally have antecedents. However, when they are in isolated sentences, the antecedent will often be missing. Antecedents can also come after the pronoun.

Exercise 67

Directions: Underline the pronoun and then write its antecedent.

Example: My mother cooked lunch for <u>her</u> neighbors.   *mother*

1. The officer gave his friend a ticket. _____

2. Mary lost her sweater in the rain. _____

3. Jerry gave his sister flowers. _____

4. Carlos wants me to give him my report. _____

5. The team lost its way to the game. _____

6. We all left our shoes outside the temple. _____

7. Miguel gave his money to the church. _____

8. Marilyn and her friends sent their money to charity. _____

9. The manager of the store gave his workers a raise. _____

10. Jim and his wife spent their savings to buy a farm. _____

11. My friends planned their first party for next month. _____

12. Tom returned his book to the library. _____

76

13. Sally gave her sister a bracelet. _____

14. Sylvia put her donations in the basket. _____

15. Joe found his book in the principal's office. _____

16. Lois read the accusations and denied them. _____

17. Grace gave her sister a pair of skates. _____

18. My brother found his wallet in the alley. _____

19. Joan took good care of her little sister. _____

20. Jerry fixed his computer. _____

Personal Pronouns

Personal pronouns refer to a person or a thing. Because they refer to nouns they must agree with the nouns in gender and number. They are almost always in the same form as the noun to which they refer. Masculine nouns take masculine pronouns; feminine nouns take feminine pronouns. Singular nouns take singular pronouns; plural nouns take plural pronouns. In the examples below, the antecedent and correct reference are underlined. Note that the pronoun agrees with the antecedent, not with the noun it modifies.

<u>Ted</u> needed <u>his</u> car for work.
His is masculine singular.

<u>He</u> needed <u>his</u> car for work.
He and *his* are masculine singular.

<u>Therese</u> enjoys <u>her</u> work.
Her is feminine singular.

<u>She</u> enjoys <u>her</u> work.
She and *her* are feminine singular.

<u>Max</u> and <u>Lisa</u> left <u>their</u> papers.
Their is plural.

<u>They</u> left <u>their</u> papers.
They and *their* are plural.

Uses of Pronouns

Personal Pronouns as Subjects
Memorize the personal pronouns for subjects.

	Singular	Plural
First person	I	we
Second person	you	you
Third person	he, she, it	they

We found the books behind the shelf.

The subject of this sentence is *we*.

Exercise 68

Directions: Complete the following sentences with the correct subjective pronouns.

Example: *She* wants a new sweater.   (third person singular feminine)

1. _____ plan to visit my father in Idaho. (first person singular)

2. _____ enjoyed the play *The King and I.* (first person plural)

3. _____ promised to help us decorate the classroom. (third person plural)

4. _____ must see that show. (second person singular)

5. _____ plans to leave later. (third person singular masculine)

6. _____ participated in the panel. (third person singular feminine)

7. _____ could not be recognized. (third person singular neuter)

8. _____ cannot go with you. (first person singular)

9. _____ were amused by his jokes. (first person plural)

10. _____ should win top honors.   (third person singular feminine)

11. _____ joined the choir. (third person plural)

12. _____ will go swimming. (first person plural)

13. _____ saw a beautiful sunset. (first person singular)

14. _____ need a vacation. (second person singular)

15. _____ studies Latin. (third person singular masculine)

Personal Pronouns after Linking Verbs

Linking verbs never express action. They make a statement by connecting the subject with a word in the predicate that explains or describes the subject. Pronouns following a linking verb use the same form as the subject. (This form is called *case.*)

The <u>actor</u> was <u>he</u>.   He was the actor.
subject   subjective personal pronoun

Marlene will be the secretary.   Marlene will be she.

Betsy is a make-up artist.   Betsy is she.

Although this construction is correct, note that the objective case is often used after the linking verb in conversation and for emphasis. Many people avoid the awkward sound of "It is I."

Directions: Underline the linking verbs. Then write a correct personal pronoun in the blank.

Example: The player <u>was</u> *he*.

Note that this sentence is correct, but most English speakers would *begin* the sentence with the pronoun.

1. The girl must have been _____ .

2. The best quarterback was _____ .

3. It was _____ in the room.

4. It could have been _____ on the stage.

5. The most talented boy was _____ .

6. The most popular cheerleaders were_____ .

7. It was _____ acting on the stage.

8. The leaders could be _____ .

9. The members on the team were _____ .

10. The victim must have been _____ .

Personal Pronouns as Objects
Memorize the personal pronouns for objects.

	Singular	**Plural**
First person	me	us
Second person	you	you
Third person	him, her, it	them

Direct Object
Use objective pronouns after verbs that ask *what* or *whom*.

We	saw	them	at the store.
subject		*direct object (whom?)*	

The girls	recognized	us.
subject		*direct object*

Exercise 70

Directions: Label the underlined pronouns *S* for subject or *DO* for direct object.

Example: <u>You</u> left the coat there.   *S*

_____ 1.   They took <u>us</u> to the show.

_____ 2.   <u>We</u> returned home, wet and hungry.

_____ 3.   Jerry saw <u>him</u> at the store.

_____ 4.   The lady called <u>us.</u>

_____ 5.   Joan asked <u>her</u> for help.

_____ 6.   <u>You</u> sent Tom on that errand.

_____ 7.   The bus took <u>us</u> to the game.

_____ 8.   <u>She</u> is a great pianist.

_____ 9.   Leave <u>him</u> alone.

_____ 10.   My mother sent <u>us</u> to the store.

_____ 11.   Jerry and <u>I</u> like to play basketball.

_____ 12.   The storm frightened <u>you</u>.

_____ 13.   Julie asked <u>them</u> for the package.

_____ 14.   <u>She</u> was the winner.

_____ 15.   Did <u>you</u> go to the show?

_____ 16.   <u>We</u> enjoyed the concert.

_____ 17.   <u>It</u> will be an unusual event.

_____ 18.   Her friend found <u>her</u> at the mall.

_____ 19.   Is it surely <u>he</u> on the tennis court?

_____ 20.   The storm injured <u>him</u>.

Exercise 71

Directions: Write a pronoun to replace the underlined words.

Example: <u>My</u> <u>sister</u> and <u>her</u> <u>friends</u> brought sandwiches.   *They*

1.   <u>Jerry</u> <u>and</u> <u>Tom</u> went camping.   _____

2.   I saw <u>Sue</u> at the movie.   _____

3.   The best player was <u>Joe</u>.   _____

4.   Mary blamed <u>Sue</u> <u>and</u> <u>Joan</u> for the accident.   _____

5.   The cop warned <u>Lou</u> <u>and</u> <u>Bill</u> about the danger.   _____

6. The best soccer players were <u>Joe</u> <u>and</u> <u>Pat</u>. _____

7. The news baffled <u>Chuck</u>. _____

8. <u>Janet</u> plays tennis. _____

9. It was <u>Bob</u> <u>and</u> <u>Dave</u> in the car. _____

10. The most talented actress is <u>Jean</u>. _____

11. It must have been <u>Mario</u> in the gym. _____

12. Everyone saw <u>Lee</u> <u>and</u> <u>Al</u> playing tennis. _____

13. <u>Mike</u> gave a party last night. _____

14. The <u>teacher</u> gave Tom a demerit. _____

15. <u>Larry</u> dropped his wallet while shopping. _____

16. <u>Alice</u> <u>and</u> <u>Sue</u> joined the basketball team. _____

17. In the meadow <u>bees</u> buzzed loudly. _____

18. <u>Children</u> enjoy games. _____

19. Another favorite character is <u>Donald</u> <u>Duck</u>. _____

20. Most people enjoy <u>a</u> <u>murder</u> <u>mystery</u>. _____

Exercise 72

Directions: Underline the correct pronoun.

Example: Tell (she, <u>her</u>) that I called.

1. I saw (they, them) at the game.

2. (We, Us) sent them the equipment.

3. Bob and (she, her) plan to go to college.

4. Lisa and (I, me) went for a joyride.

5. It must be (they, them) asking for a raise.

6. Give (we, us) the report.

7. Notify (they, them) about our change of address.

8. Was (she, her) the first to win?

9. Sally called Tim and (I, me) about the job.

10. Barb and (he, him) made the team.

11. The coach encouraged (I, me) to go to camp.

12. The guide urged (we, us) to hurry.

13. The map showed (they, them) the way.

14. The principal recommended Michelle and (I, me).

15. Give (he, him) first choice.

16. The guide left (she, her) behind.

17. Do you expect (they, them) to arrive today?

18. Let (we, us) come with you.

19. Mr. Jones took Jack, Pete, and (I, me) to the rodeo.

20. You can follow (they, them) on the hike.

Exercise 73

Directions: Label the pronouns *S* for subject or *O* for object.

Example: he *S*

_____ 1. me

_____ 2. I

_____ 3. him

_____ 4. her

_____ 5. them

_____ 6. they

_____ 7. us

_____ 8. we

_____ 9. she

_____ 10. he

Exercise 74

Directions: Underline the correct pronoun. If the phrase does not begin with a verb, the noun/pronoun combination is the subject.

Example: ask (he, <u>him</u>)

1. Bob and (I, me)

2. noticed (we, us)

3. Jerry and (he, him)

4. Bob and (they, them)

5. showed (I, me)

6. frightened (they, them)

7. chose (I, me)

8. Mary and (we, us)

9. pleased Lois and (we, us)

10. called (we, us)

11. saw (they, them)

12. believed (him, she)

13. asked (him, she)

14. took (me, I)

15. hired Susie and (she, her)

16. asked (we, us)

17. Joe and (I, me)

18. she and (they, them)

19. she and (he, him)

20. introduced (he, him)

Exercise 75

Directions: Use the phrases in **Exercise 74** to write original sentences.

Exercise 76

Directions: Underline the correct pronoun. Circle any linking verbs.

Example: The next class president (will be) (she, her).

1. Was (she, her) the best writer?

2. After traveling fifty miles, my brother and (she, her) stopped for a bite to eat.

3. Marie and (they, them) enjoyed their trip.

4. It could have been (he, him) in that picture.

5. Everyone saw (we, us) at the party.

6. Would (he, him) be the most popular teacher?

7. It was (I, me) in that accident.

8. The helicopter and (he, him) were not found.

9. The pilot and (she, her) were good friends.

10. I saw Tom and (they, them) at the circus.

11. Will (she, her) be the next batter?

12. Joe and (I, me) went to the game.

13. The teacher named (she, her) the best writer.

14. The coach praised (she, her) for winning the game.

15. Peter and (we, us) will go skiing this winter.

16. (We, Us) need your help.

17. The villain in the play was (he, him).

18. Give (we, us) the news.

19. Send (she, her) the card.

20. (We, Us) will play soccer.

Exercise 77

Directions: The following underlined pronouns are correct. Explain why.

Example: We asked <u>them</u> for the tickets. Them *is the objective pronoun used after a verb that asks the question* whom.

1.   My mother took James and <u>me</u> to a rodeo.

2.   The usher gave <u>us</u> programs.

3.   A guide took Jane and <u>her</u> backstage.

4.   Father called <u>me</u> to the phone.

5.   The man hired Suzie and <u>him</u> to run errands.

6.   The new members are Joan and <u>she</u>.

7.   <u>We</u> plan to leave next week for Florida.

8.   The teacher chose <u>us</u> three to go.

9.   The neighbors and <u>they</u> are planning a block party.

10. The pilot and <u>he</u> made a safe landing.

Indirect Object

Like nouns, pronouns can also be used as indirect objects.

I gave Al and him the books.
I gave the books to him.

Exercise 78

Directions: Underline the correct pronoun.

Example: Did (<u>he</u>, him) know where the letter is?

1. Give Carlos or (I, me) the article.

2. We sent (he, him) the notice yesterday.

3. My mother made (she, her) a cake.

4. Provide Larry and (he, him) with the necessary equipment.

5. We gave Simon and (they, them) a picnic at the beach.

6. The pilot gave (we, us) a ride in his plane.

7. The pitcher threw Ted and (I, me) a fast ball.

8. The policeman gave Maude and (she, her) a ticket.

9. We bought Al and (they, them) a lunch.

10. Please give (we, us) an advanced notice.

11. We sent (they, them) the books.

12. The class sent (she, her) a get-well card.

13. The coach gave Bob and (he, him) the honors.

14. They mailed James and (he, him) the report.

15. The principal gave (she, her) the medal.

16. The news of the accident made (we, us) unhappy.

17. The saleslady sold Mary and (I, me) two sweaters.

18. Bob sent Irma and (I, me) a copy of his play.

19. Miss Jones made (her, she) the costume for the play.

20. The actors sent (we, us) notices of their play.

Exercise 79

Directions: Underline the correct pronoun in the following sentences.

Example: They asked (we, <u>us</u>) how to find the park.

1. (We, Us) lost the way to the gym.

2. We found Pete and (he, him) happy over the outcome.

3. It must have been (she, her) at the concert.

4. We followed (he, him).

5. (I, me) was delighted with the turnout.

6. The man blamed (we, us) for the accident.

7. Please send (she, her) this note.

8. The professor gave (I, me) the specimen.

9. They managed to keep (we, us) in suspense.

10. Were (we, us) the ones responsible?

11. The surprise made (they, them) happy.

12. (They, them) want the news immediately.

13. They sent Bob and (they, them) the money.

14. Was (he, him) a fighter?

15. John and (he, him) were good friends.

16. (We, Us) passed the test.

17. The guard took (she, her) home.

18. The spectators placed (we, us) at the scene of the accident.

19. Did you see (they, them) during the party?

20. (They, Them) want the news immediately.

Interrogative and Demonstrative Pronouns

Interrogative pronouns ask questions. They ask *who, whom, which, what,* and *whose.*

The interrogative pronouns that cause problems are *who* and *whom.* Who is always used for subjects and whom is always used for objects.

> Who is coming with you to the party?
> You saw whom?

Exercise 80

Directions: Underline the correct pronoun.

Example: The best actor was (<u>who</u>, whom)?

1. (Who, Whom) wrote the Bill of Rights?

2. To (who, whom) did you give that book?

3. (Who, Whom) did you see yesterday?

4. (Who, Whom) will be visiting you next month?

5. (Who, Whom) will be captain of the volleyball team next year?

6. The participants were (who, whom)?

7. About (who, whom) did she speak?

8. (Who, Whom) did she consult about the illness?

9. For (who, whom) did you buy this bracelet?

10. (Who, Whom) will be in the tennis tournament?

Demonstrative pronouns are *this, that, these,* and *those.* These pronouns are used to point out one or more nouns. *This* and *that* are singular; *these* and *those* are plural.

> That is my essay.
>
> These paints belong to me.
>
> Those articles were in his desk drawer.
>
> This belongs in the library.

Note

Demonstrative pronouns seldom cause problems. You should be able to recognize them as pronouns.

Indefinite Pronouns

Indefinite pronouns refer to persons, places, or things without specifying which ones. They don't require specific antecedents, but they can have them.

Singular Indefinite Pronouns

The following indefinite pronouns are always singular and take a singular verb. Memorize these pronouns. This concept is very important.

> each   every   either   neither
>
> one (anyone, someone, no one)
>
> body (everybody, nobody, somebody)
>
> thing (anything, everything, something)
>
> Each of the books on the shelf has been bought by my grandfather.

The subject is *each* (singular); the verb is also singular.

> Everybody is welcome.
>
> Not one of these jackets fits me.
>
> Nothing escapes him.

Exercise 81

Directions: Underline the correct verb and circle the indefinite pronoun.

Example: (No one) (<u>was</u>, were) at the meeting.

1. Each of the papers on the table (was, were) corrected yesterday.

2. Not one of the examples given (is, are) correct.

3. Anything (is, are) possible tonight.

4. No one (was, were) eligible for the contest.

5. Either of the teams (have, has) a good reputation.

6. Neither of the dishes (have, has) ever been broken.

7. Anyone (is, are) eligible to try out in the essay contest.

8. Anybody (has, have) a chance to win the prize.

9. Each of the projects (was, were) well represented.

10. Not one of the dishes (was, were) broken.

11. Neither of the girls (was, were) present at school today.

12. Neither of the balls (have, has) been stolen.

13. Nobody in the class (report, reports) any misconduct.

14. Everyone in the room (sing, sings) in the choir.

15. Nothing (is, are) accomplished without hard work.

16. Neither of the twins (has, have) filled out her application for college.

17. No one (was, were) admitted after 9:00 P.M.

18. Not one of the candidates (is, are) qualified.

19. Each of his answers (is, are) accurate.

20. According to our records, nothing (was, were) lost.

Plural Indefinite Pronouns

Some indefinite pronouns are always plural and take a plural verb. They are *several, few, both, many,* and *others.* Memorize these pronouns.

> Several of the books were ruined by the rain.
>
> Both the pies were eaten.
>
> Only a few of these projects were successful.
>
> Many balls were missing.

Some indefinite pronouns can be singular or plural depending on the phrase that follows. They are *all, any, most, more,* and *some.* Memorize these pronouns.

> Some of the apples were spoiled. Some of the apple was rotten.
>
> All of the work is done. All of the papers are corrected.
>
> Most of the projects were missing. All the boys are assembled.

Exercise 82

Directions: Underline the correct verb.

Example: Most of the work (<u>was,</u> were) finished.

1. Several days in April (was, were) very rainy.

2. All of the parcels (has, have) been shipped.

3. Some of the boys in the room (is, are) having problems.

4. Both of the trips (is, are) expensive.

5. Neither of the answers (is, are) correct.

6. Several of the debates (was, were) very good.

7. Most of the letters (was, were) written by children.

8. Any of those articles (is, are) for sale.

9. (Is, Are) everything marked for sale tomorrow?

10. Most of the pizza (was, were) eaten.

11. Did any of the articles (interest, interests) you?

12. One of the papers on the board (is, are) mine.

13. Not one of the candidates (has, have) really been successful.

14. (Has, Have) anyone been appointed treasurer?

15. Most of the pages in the book (was, were) destroyed.

16. (Has, Have) anyone completed his project?

17. None of my friends (play, plays) soccer.

18. Several reports (is, are) missing.

19. (Is, Are) everything mentioned in the report?

20. Everyone (was, were) invited to the celebration.

21. Neither of them (want, wants) to have company.

22. Both of the athletes (enjoy, enjoys) skiing.

23. All of the newspapers (carry, carries) the story.

24. Everyone (decide, decides) for himself.

25. Some of the cars (are, is) air-conditioned.

26. Both of these sweaters (cost, costs) the same.

27. A few of these TV shows (pass, passes) the time.

28. One of these magazines (have, has) good recipes.

29. Some of the track (has, have) been repaired.

30. Everybody (enjoy, enjoys) a good time.

Possessive Pronouns

Memorize the following possessive pronouns.

my, mine	our, ours
your, yours	your, yours
his, hers (her), its	their, theirs

Notes

Many of these possessive pronouns function as adjectives because they are used to limit the meaning of a noun.

my book	his bike	my parents

In this book we classify them as pronouns.

Never use the apostrophe with personal pronouns. Possessive pronouns already show ownership.

Correct

hers	yours	ours

The apostrophe is used with *indefinite* pronouns.

> It was nobody's business.
>
> Everybody's wishes were fulfilled.

Directions: Underline the possessive pronouns.

Example: Is that your coat?

1. The book is mine.

2. The basketball is theirs.

3. That car is hers.

4. It was his to begin with.

5. Did you enjoy his talk?

6. That scooter is faster than ours.

7. The prize is his.

8. Its wing was broken.

9. Her car was vandalized.

10. Her computer won't work.

11. She can use my book.

12. That project is mine.

13. Its rim was made of gold.

14. Ours is better than yours.

15. The victory is not theirs.

16. Her talk was boring.

17. Her face has lost its youthfulness.

18. Their flight was delayed.

19. That dog is ours.

20. Your allegations are unfounded.

Pronouns and Contractions

Possessive personal pronouns already show ownership. They never need an apostrophe. An apostrophe is used for contractions.

> they are   they're
>
> she will not   she won't

Its means ownership.

> The book was in its place on the table.

It's is a contraction meaning it is.

> It's too late to turn in your paper.

Directions: Write the correct word in the space provided.

Example: *You're* the new student council representative. (You're, Your)

1. _____ too early to leave. (It's, Its)

2. _____nest was destroyed by the wind. (It's, Its)

3. _____ beak was chipped. (It's, Its)

4. _____ our new substitute teacher. (You're, Your)

5. The book is Sally's. The book is _____ (her, hers).

6. _____ too late to decide. (It's, Its)

7. The material belonged to my parents. It was _____ (their, theirs).

8. We noticed_____ leg was broken. (it's, its)

9. _____ a little late to register. (It's, Its)

10. The report belonged to us. It was_____ (ours, our).

11. _____ time to mail your application. (It's, Its)

12. _____ a new bike. (It's, Its)

13. _____ really a fun project. (It's, Its)

14. We like_____ singing. (your, you're)

15. _____ feeding jar has disappeared. (It's, Its)

16. _____ my pleasure to join you. (It's, Its)

17. Maria's project is better. _____ is better (Hers, Her).

18. _____ not raining today. (It's, Its)

19. _____ an interesting story. (It's, Its)

20. _____ place was taken. (It's. Its)

21. That book does not belong to us. It is not _____ (our, ours).

22. _____ too late to decide. (It's, Its)

23. _____ wing was injured. (It's, Its)

24. _____ time to leave. (It's, Its)

25. _____ just the news. (It's, Its)

Unit 4 Review

1. A pronoun is a word that takes the place of a noun or refers to a noun.

2. An antecedent is the noun or nouns to which a pronoun refers.

3. Personal pronouns refer to persons or things. They must agree with their antecedent in number (singular or plural) and gender (masculine, feminine, neuter), but not in usage (subject, object).

4. Personal pronouns as subjects:

    I, you, he, she, it, we, you, them

    Personal pronouns are used as subjects or following a linking verb.

5. Personal pronouns as objects:

    a. Direct object

        Personal pronouns used as direct objects follow a verb and can answer the questions *what* or *whom.*

    b. Indirect object

        Personal pronouns can answer the questions *to* or *for whom* something is given. An indirect object comes before a direct object.

6. Interrogative pronouns ask a question. They are *who, whom, which, what,* and *whose.* Who is always used as a subject or after a linking verb. Whom is always an indirect or direct object.

7. Demonstrative pronouns point out one or more nouns. They are *this, that, these,* and *those.*

8. Indefinite Pronouns.

    a. Singular indefinite pronouns

        each, every, neither, either, one, body, thing

    b. Plural indefinite pronouns

        several, few, both, many, others

    c. Singular or plural indefinite pronouns

        all, any, most, more, some

    The number that is assumed depends on the prepositional phrase that follows the pronoun.

9. Possessive Pronouns

        my, mine, your, yours, his, her, hers, its, our, ours, their, theirs

    Never use the apostrophe with possessive pronouns to show ownership. Only use an apostrophe with personal pronouns to show a contraction, that is to show that a letter or letters have been omitted.

Unit 4
Review Test

Part A.

Directions: Underline the pronoun and write its antecedent on the line.

1. Liz left her bike at school. _____

2. The girls gave their coach flowers. _____

3. Mary asked the guard for her passport. _____

4. My friends gave up their lunch money. _____

5. The books had lost their covers. _____

6. Most of the fruit had lost its flavor. _____

7. Peter gave his passport to the guard. _____

8. The boss gave his employees a bonus. _____

9. Jane gave me her math book. _____

10. Rose gave her book to my sister. _____

Part B.

Directions: Underline the correct pronoun.

1. The test should cause (he, him) no difficulty.

2. The best scholars are Jane and (she, her).

3. Were Brian and (he, him) the contestants?

4. (They, Them) will plan the menu for the party.

5. Marian and (we, us) have difficulty organizing that dance.

6. Jon and his brother sent (they, them) an invitation.

7. Did you see (we, us) yesterday?

8. The teacher asked Carter and (he, him) to help.

9. My mother saw (they, them) in the room.

10. Was it (they, them) at the theater?

Part C.

Directions: Underline the correct verbs.

1. Several bills (was, were) rejected.

2. Each of his proposals (was, were) acceptable.

3. (Have, Has) either of the orders been sent?

4. Nobody (want, wants) to accept the blame.

5. Several of his friends (is, are) joining the air force.

6. Everybody (give, gives) to the Red Cross.

7. Either Tom or his sister (is, are) representing the school.

8. Not one of the spectators (blame, blames) the coach.

9. Anybody (is, are) free to apply.

10. Some of these apples (is, are) not fit to eat.

Part D.

Directions: Write *S* if the underlined pronoun is a subject, *DO* if it is a direct object, or *IO* if it is an indirect object.

_____ 1. <u>We</u> girls will do the job.

_____ 2. Did Jane see <u>them</u> at the movie?

_____ 3. Albert gave <u>me</u> a certificate for ice cream.

_____ 4. Are you sure it was <u>they</u>?

_____ 5. This may be <u>he</u> coming down the walk.

_____ 6. Carol gave <u>them</u> the message.

_____ 7. Michelle will be inviting <u>them</u> to the party.

_____ 8. Sally always blames <u>us</u> for mistakes.

_____ 9. The coach chose Carmen and <u>me</u>.

_____ 10. I told <u>her</u> a story about Christmas.

_____ 11. Was that <u>she</u> in the room?

_____ 12. My parents and <u>they</u> are arriving later.

_____ 13. Did you tell <u>me</u> the truth?

_____ 14. Were <u>we</u> the ones you wanted?

_____ 15. When do you expect <u>her</u> to arrive?

_____ 16. Please send <u>them</u> the tickets.

_____ 17. Did you know it was <u>she</u>?

_____ 18. The debate team sent Jim and <u>him</u> a challenge.

_____ 19. My father bought <u>her</u> a typewriter

_____ 20. Mary and <u>I</u> do not need your advice.

Part E.

Directions: Underline the correct possessive pronoun or contraction.

1. (You're, Your) singing is better than Mary's.

2. (It's, Its) too late to even try.

3. (It's, Its) pride was hurt.

4. (You're, Your) not planning to quit now?

5. (It's, Its) a foolish guess.

A **preposition** occurs before a noun or pronoun and expresses a relationship between it and another word in the sentence.

The car raced down the street.

The preposition *down* shows the relationship of car and street.

Tom took his sister to the show.

The preposition *to* shows the relationship of sister and show.

Exercise 85

Directions: Underline the prepositions and write the nouns they are relating.

Example: The dog ran <u>around</u> the house.   *dog, house*

1.   The boys walked to the store.   _____

2.   The house was made of adobe.   _____

3.   She saw the dogs in the window.   _____

4.   The man came toward John.   _____

5.   I visited the museum with Larry.   _____

6.   In anger Pete ran out of the house.   _____

7.   The little boy climbed up the ladder.   _____

8.   The tools are outside the garage.   _____

9.   Molly climbed over the fence.   _____

10. He could see the parade from his seat.   _____

11. Jane walked to school.   _____

12. Her ball rolled down the drain.   _____

13. The cards were on the table.   _____

14. I visited the museum with her.   _____

15. The little girl ran out of the house.   _____

16. Ralph walked slowly down the stairs.   _____

17. The bowl of jelly refused to jell.   _____

18. The boys ran to the beach.   _____

19. He dived under the waves.   _____

20. She was soon covered with sand.   _____

The best way to recognize prepositions is to become familiar with the most common ones. Some prepositions have more than one word. These are sometimes called **compound prepositions**. There are many prepositions. These listed below are just a few.

about	beyond	in regard to	regarding
above	by	inside	round
according to	concerning	into	through
across	down	like	till
after	during	near	to
along	except	of	toward
among	for	off	under
at	from	on	until
below	in	out	up
beneath	in back of	outside	upon
beside	in front of	over	with

Prepositional Phrases

Prepositions are always part of a group of words called a **prepositional phrase**. A prepositional phrase begins with a preposition and ends with a noun or pronoun. A preposition can never stand alone in a sentence. It is always used with a noun or pronoun that is called the **object of the preposition**. Prepositional phrases can have more than one object. The objects may have modifiers.

> She gave a treat to Tom.

To Tom is a prepositional phrase. *Tom* is the object of the preposition, *to*.

> Mother looked under the couch and the chair for the lost pen.

Couch and *chair* are both objects of the preposition *under.*

> The earthquake happened during the mystery movie.

Mystery modifies *movie,* which is the object of the preposition *during.*

Prepositions change the relationship in a sentence.

> The ball rolled toward Jim.
> The ball rolled across the street and into the park.
> The ball rolled down the street.
> The ball rolled on the grass and into a hole.

Exercise 86

Directions: Underline the prepositions in the following sentences.

Example: She posted the map <u>on</u> the wall.

1. Tom jogged across the street and into the apartment.

2. The baseball rolled across the field.

3. The passengers stayed in their rooms during the storm.

4. Do not walk on the freshly planted grass.

5. Everyone enjoyed the talk by Professor Goldstein.

6. Colonial costumes were among the valuable treasures in the museum.

7. Luis walked slowly over the leaves from the old oak tree.

8. Everyone left early except Tom.

9. She sent the report to the judge.

10. The clock in our kitchen is broken.

11. The plane flew over the ocean and through the clouds.

12. A bird outside my window kept me awake.

13. Frustrated, Molly threw down her pen and walked out of the room.

14. Practice was scheduled on Monday for all track members.

15. There are many historic landmarks in the West.

16. There was bickering among the girls during the play.

17. A bear visited our tent, walked around it, and then ambled off.

18. My sister got off her horse and ran toward the stable.

19. We found a treasure underneath our house.

20. My dog crawled under the fence.

Exercise 87

Directions: Add an appropriate preposition to complete the sentences below.

Example: She kicked the ball *onto* the roof.

1. My sister bought cereal _____ the store.

2. My friend and I walked _____ the river.

3. A mysterious package was lying _____ the table.

4. Dave watched the rain_____ his window.

5. The car raced _____ the track and into the wall.

6. The sun shone _____ the surface of the lake.

7. Put your shoes _____ the bed.

8. The flowers were placed _____ the fountain.

9. The paper airplane sailed _____ the park.

10. The earthquake occurred_____ my final examination.

Every preposition must have an object. Without an object, the word is not a preposition.

Directions: Underline the prepositions and put parentheses around the objects of the prepositions.

Example: The box of (oranges) was on the floor.

1. The boys on the soccer team went by bus to Mammoth.

2. A man with several pamphlets in his hand knocked on our door.

3. The window in my room was smashed by a baseball.

4. Our air conditioner broke during the hottest day of the year.

5. Lee took several books to the library for his mother.

6. The dogs chased each other around the park.

7. Our house is located next to the golf course and behind the parking lot.

8. Entering her apartment, Carol took off her coat and shoes, poured a drink from the refrigerator, and sank into her favorite recliner.

9. Alisha skied easily down the slopes and through the dense pine trees.

10. The price of the Mercury was too high for my income.

11. Dave, my cousin from Chicago, came to San Francisco for his vacation.

12. The fight between Tom and me ended with a truce.

13. I witnessed the accident from my bedroom window.

14. My mother planned a fabulous birthday party for me and my friends.

15. Our class sent a get-well card to Paul, who is in the hospital with a broken leg.

16. Something in the corner of my room moved quickly along the wall and into my bathroom.

17. During the storm, Jane closed the windows in the living room and bedrooms.

18. The cartons of milk in the sun turned sour by lunchtime.

19. Larry ran to the backyard and took his scooter out of the rain.

20. After school we went to the store for some ice cream.

Objects of Prepositions

When pronouns are used as objects of a preposition, they must be in the objective case.

> We gave the book to her.

The pronoun *her* is the object of the preposition *to*.

Exercise 89

Directions: The following sentences are correct. Briefly explain the use of each underlined pronoun.

Example: The story is about <u>him</u>.
The pronoun him *is the object of the preposition* about.

1.   The secret is between you and <u>him</u>.

2.   The teacher placed Ken, a new student, next to <u>her</u>.

3.   We waited for Bruce and <u>him</u> to join us at the show.

4.   We sent the get-well card to <u>her</u>.

5.   Between the fire fighters and <u>us</u> there was a feeling of relief.

6.   According to <u>him</u>, there is nothing to worry about.

7.   All the students went on a field trip except <u>me</u>.

8.   Sally sat behind <u>her</u> for the entire year.

9.   Our new house is near my friend and <u>them</u>.

10. He liked to keep his friends around <u>him</u>.

Exercise 90

Directions: Write sentences using the following prepositional phrases.

1.   like you and me

2.   before Fred and her

3.   except Mary and him

4.   beside Sally and them

5.   between Albert and him

6.   from his cousin and her

7.   behind our parents and them

8.   for them

9.   without me

10. around her

11. after Tom and him

12. according to Joe and us

13. for Ted and me

14. to the teacher and her

15. about Anita and them

16. with Bob and us

17. toward us

18. among them

19. to Jerry and us

20. like him

Distinguishing between Indirect Objects and Objects of a Preposition

The indirect object always comes before the direct object and the *to* and *for* are understood. With the object of a preposition, the *to* and *for* are always in the sentence.

> Her sister gave her the wristwatch.
>
> Her sister gave (*to* is understood) her the wristwatch.
> *Indirect object*
>
> Her sister gave the wristwatch to her.
> *Object of a preposition*

Exercise 91

Directions: Change each indirect object into a prepositional phrase, and each prepositional phrase into an indirect object.

Example: I gave a reward to him. *I gave him a reward.*

1. My friend sent Bob and me an invitation to his birthday party.

2. I gave my guests beautiful souvenirs.

3. The salesman showed us two beautiful bracelets.

4. Jack promised an award to Alice.

5. Did you make that dress for Mary?

6. I gave my friend a ticket for the Lakers game.

7. The attendant left us a message.

8. The policeman gave me a ticket for speeding.

9. The coach sent us a wedding invitation.

10. Did you bring ice cream for the children?

Directions: Underline the indirect objects. Then change the indirect objects to objects of a preposition.

Example: We left <u>Sam</u> a note. *We left a note for Sam.*

1. The teacher gave Becky a good grade.

2. The nurse gives her patients good care.

3. Librarians find students research material.

4. My friend gave me flowers for my birthday.

5. She sent him the package.

6. We offered them our special assistance.

7. The teacher gave her students a list of rules.

8. The clerks send borrowers overdue notices.

9. The committee gave the winners special medals.

10. School counselors offer teachers and students advice.

Directions: Underline the correct answer.

Example: All of the cards belong to Mike and (he, <u>him</u>).

1. Dolores sat near Bob and (I, me).

2. The lady made that dress for (she, her).

3. We sent all the material to Bob and (they, them).

4. We talked with the counselor, the parents, and (they, them).

5. Behind Paula and (we, us) were the audience.

6. The report was signed by Joy and (he, him).

7. They left early except Jerry and (we, us).

8. The picture really looked like (she, her).

9. My mother sat beside (I, me) at the concert.

10. Give that book to (he, him).

11. Please be with (we, us) at the trial.

12. The librarian awarded reading prizes to Barbara and (she, her).

13. His boss was angry with (he, him).

14. The guide will give much information to (they, them).

15. The principal gave a copy of the rules to (we, us).

16. The dogs began leaping around Sara and (I, me).

17. I bought a pizza for Isabel and (she, her).

18. Thomas walked between (we, us) girls.

19. The guard turned his head toward Irene and (we, us).

20. Please wait for Ed and (they, them) at the gym.

Exercise 94

Directions: Underline the prepositional phrases in the following paragraph.

The Knights of the Round Table is a term descriptive of those knights who had places around King Arthur's banquet table. King Arthur used the round table to prevent jealousy over seating precedence and to symbolize the equality of the knights. It was believed that 130 knights had places at the round table, but there may have been more. Generally, however, only those knights of most conspicuous importance have come to be regarded as the Knights of the Round Table.

Exercise 95

Directions: Write a paragraph describing an organization. Underline the prepositional phrases in your paragraph.

Unit 5 Review

1. A preposition relates a noun or pronoun with another word in the sentence.

2. Prepositions are always part of a group of words called a prepositional phrase. A prepositional phrase begins with a preposition and ends with a noun or pronoun. A preposition can never stand alone in a sentence.

3. Prepositions can have more than one object and may have modifiers.

4. The object of a preposition is always in the objective form of the pronoun (the objective case). Always use the objective case after a preposition.

5. The indirect object always comes before the direct object and the *to* and *for* are always understood. In prepositional phrases, the *to* and *for* are always in the sentence.

Part A.

Directions: Underline the prepositions in the following sentences.

1. Jane practices the violin before a concert.

2. Many of the tourists enjoy small towns.

3. A visit to the desert is an unusual experience.

4. Sara practices at home for hours.

5. Sam spoke about his work.

6. He had to stay after school for his own good.

7. The storm kept me at home.

8. We all laughed at the joke.

9. Molly is endowed with a generous nature.

10. Jim accomplished his goal by fair means.

Part B.

Directions: Add an appropriate preposition.

1. Jim walked _____ town.

2. The field was irrigated_____ a system of canals.

3. Jane was always true _____ her word.

4. Leaves_____ the tree littered the lawn.

5. We all left the room_____ Paul.

6. We divided the flowers _____ the three of us.

7. _____ John and Ralph there was no friendship.

8. Sally had a serious talk _____ her brother.

9. They went _____ the house quietly.

10. My father likes to stay _____ home.

Part C.

Directions: Underline the preposition and put parentheses around the object.

1. The girls in my class are all good students.

2. Bob crawled over the fence and through the field.

3. During the war, many wonderful men died.

4. The water from the last rain is still underneath our house.

5. We invited everyone except Peter to the barbecue.

6. The man walked into the classroom, looked around the room, and walked out.

7. We ran into the ocean and shouted for joy.

8. It happened during the last game.

9. Becky loves walking in the sand and playing in the mud.

10. The display of artwork in the art department was an inspiration to everyone.

Part D.

Directions: Underline the correct pronouns and put parentheses around all prepositions.

1. She wanted to give a TV to (she, her) for Mother's Day.

2. Will you please send a sample of your artwork to (I, me).

3. She will graduate after (he, him).

4. Are you waiting for Jim and (she, her)?

5. The height of the building was measured by Kelly and (he, him).

6. Are you going to leave with (we, us)?

7. Frank came to the movie after Jan and (I, me).

8. Would you make a costume for Jack and (she, her)?

9. The task was assigned to Juanita and (he, him).

10. The argument is between (we, us).

11. Give the video to (they, them).

12. She was sitting near Marsha and (he, him).

13. My mother has been asking about you and (they, them).

14. Please send your opinion to (we, us).

15. I refuse to go with (he, him).

16. There would be no agreement among Maria, Josh, and (she, her).

17. My dad bought a computer for my brother and (I, me).

18. There was a serious disagreement between the senator and (we, us).

19. She left the party after (he, him).

20. You should have sent the material to (he, him) or (they, them).

Unit 6
Adjectives

What Is an Adjective?

An **adjective** is a word that describes or modifies a noun or pronoun to give the noun or pronoun a more specific meaning. The adjective brings life to a sentence, giving it interest and color. The process by which an adjective describes a word or makes it more specific is called *modification*.

dress	red dress	red, silk dress	red, silk, flowery dress
apple	yellow apple	yellow, ripe apple	golden, yellow, ripe apple

How do each of these adjectives limit the nouns *dress* and *apple*? Can you give other examples?

When you add an adjective to a noun, you immediately limit it. How do these adjectives limit the nouns?

    1. house   small house   small, white house

The adjective *small* limits a noun as to size. The adjective *white* limits a noun as to color.

2.	party	birthday party	sister's birthday party
3.	fence	wooden fence	whitewashed wooden fence
4.	room	bedroom	ivory-walled bedroom
5.	car	red car	red and black Mercury

Any word that modifies a noun is an adjective.

It can describe the noun.

            white house, ice water, yellow roses

It can state *which one?* and *what kind of?*

            first seat, fourth row, those apples

It can tell *how many?*

            two bouquets of lilies, several letters

It can state *how much?*

            enough room, little effort, no pain

Exercise 96

Directions: Underline the adjectives in the following sentences and put parentheses around the modified nouns. Do not underline articles.

Example: Her <u>gorgeous</u> (sweater) was torn at the hem.

1. A beautiful rainbow filled the sky after the heavy rain.

2. Jean went to the store and bought a blue dress and a yellow scarf.

3. Sally's green dress was a good match for her red hair.

4. Wonderful things can come in small packages.

5. Mother received a box of delicious chocolates.

6. El Nino brought torrential rains, serious floods, and devastating tornadoes.

7. We all enjoyed the delicious bread, hot and fresh from the oven.

8. For lunch we had shiny red apples.

9. My grandmother always keeps chocolate cookies in her cookie jar.

10. We went to see the wild West show last Sunday.

11. My brother sits in the fourth seat, sixth row.

12. It was a cold, windy day in January.

13. We do not need more rain.

14. Both answers will be accepted.

15. Terry spent her last quarter on a stale cookie.

16. She wrote her last paper in a hurry.

17. Did you enjoy the competitive debate between the girls and boys?

18 Sam wrote several letters to his mother.

19. The meal was delicious and colorful.

20. The sunset on the ocean is spectacular.

Articles

Articles are classified as adjectives. *The* is a **definite article** because it refers to a specific person, place or thing.

> The lawyer asked many questions.
>
> Your book is on the shelf.
>
> I studied hard for the exam.

The **indefinite articles** refer to any one of a class of persons, places, or things. The indefinite articles are *a* and *an*. Use the indefinite article *a* before consonant sounds; use *an* before vowel sounds.

> My cousin wants to be a nurse.
>
> We stayed in a hotel.
>
> She had an apple for dessert.

When the consonant *h* sounds like a vowel, use *an*.

> an honest man
>
> a humble experience

Exercise 97

Directions: Write the indefinite article needed to complete the sentence.

Example: It was *a* beautiful bouquet of roses.

1. She plays on _____ all-woman softball team.

2. The boy had only _____ apricot for lunch.

3. The teacher sent _____ book to her brother.

4. We had _____ boiled egg for breakfast.

5. Please give me _____ honest answer.

6. We rented _____ small room.

7. _____ car key is missing.

8. She was _____ only child.

9. Jeff played in _____band.

10. _____ salesman showed us several homes.

Proper Adjectives

A **proper adjective** is a proper noun used as an adjective or an adjective formed from a proper noun.

Study these capitalization rules carefully.

1. Generally proper adjectives are capitalized.

2. Do not capitalize frequently used proper adjectives.

      french fries   venetian blinds   pasteurized milk

3. Capitalize a brand name used as an adjective but do not capitalize the common noun it modifies.

      Seiko watches   Swiss cheese
      Someday you might study Joseph Conrad's novels.

4. Do not capitalize a common noun used with two proper adjectives.

      the Republican and Democratic parties.
      the Democratic Party (one proper adjective)

5. Do not capitalize prefixes attached to proper adjectives unless the prefix refers to a nationality.

      all-American   pro-Arab   Anglo-American

6. Compound adjectives are usually written as hyphenated words. In a few cases, they are written as combined words.

      far-off land   poverty-stricken people

Exercise 98

Directions: Rewrite the following sentences with correct capitalization.

Example: We rode the greyhound bus to detroit. *We rode the Greyhound bus to Detroit.*

1. That is a swiss landmark.

2. The polaroid camera, invented by edwin land, was the first instant picture camera.

3. The biblical institute attracted many people.

4. The yellowstone national park is a tourist's attraction.

5. We studied mexican art in college.

6. Ho Tan is a chinese-speaking american.

7. My friend is of anglo-french heritage.

8. Have you ever been in a chicago storm?

9. We took a cruise down the suez canal.

10. You will study english writers in high school.

11. The american way of life is sometimes admired.

12. We became interested in japanese films.

13. I hope there is a sheraton hotel in tokyo.

14. The study of elizabethan literature is most rewarding.

15. His uncle is interested in both the liberal and conservative parties.

16. Jim has an american stamp collection.

17. The pro-hispanic demonstrators marched for peace.

18. Last year I attended a brazilian festival.

19. Did you ever take an amtrak train?

20. That statue is an example of greek sculpture.

Exercise 99

Directions: Write *PA* if the sentence has proper adjectives or *CA* if it has compound adjectives.

Example: My uncle is a well-known politician.   *CA*

_____ 1.   My father does not like freeze-dried coffee.

_____ 2.   Did you ever take a Turkish bath?

_____ 3.   My friend underwent open-heart surgery last week.

_____ 4.   My grandfather had a valuable Victorian clock.

_____ 5.   Susanna always managed to keep her New York accent.

_____ 6.   Did you enjoy your Scandinavian dinner?

_____ 7.   Miguel likes to go to out-of-the-way places.

_____ 8.   The foolishness of their reactions to your questions were self-evident.

_____ 9.   The old professor was well-liked.

_____ 10.   Paul owned a waterproof parka.

Predicate Adjectives

A **predicate adjective** is an adjective that follows a linking verb and describes the subject of the sentence.

Jill was happy over the outcome of the exam.

In this sentence *happy* is an adjective describing *Jill.*

Today the waves are wild and rough.

In this sentence the predicate adjective is compound.

Exercise 100

Directions: Underline the linking verb and put parentheses around the predicate adjectives.

Example: The students <u>were</u> *(restless)* all afternoon.

1. Jaime is energetic and conscientious.

2. The girls in this class are very helpful.

3. Sara couldn't be more overjoyed at the results of her project.

4. The mystery story was very exciting.

5. The news about the tornadoes was tragic.

6. The bread is delicious.

7. The music was mournful.

8. The weather today is gloomy.

9. Sara was very sleepy from the long trip.

10. The team was exuberant over its win.

11. She is a very intelligent young lady.

12. Bill is very uncertain about his future.

13. Were you pleased with the results?

14. She can be obnoxious at times.

15. Tom has been irritable this past week.

16. My mother is fearful over the incident.

17. The bridge was almost too low for safety.

18. The gate was narrow and rough.

19. The wind was fierce this morning.

20. As a runner, Joe is fast and consistent.

Some verbs can be both action verbs and linking verbs depending on their use. The most common ones are the following:

appear	become	feel
grow	look	sound
taste	remain	smell
stay	turn	

When in doubt as to whether a verb is a linking verb or not, substitute a form of the verb *to be.*

This apple tastes sour.	Apple cannot taste. It is sour.
That lily looks fragile.	Lily cannot look. It is fragile.
I tasted the apple.	I can perform the act of tasting.
Ann looked at the lily.	Ann can perform the act of looking.

Directions: Write *L* if the verb is linking and *A* if the verb is an action verb.

Example: The blueberry pie tasted sweet. *L*

_____ 1. I felt the board on the table.

_____ 2. The man looked very angry.

_____ 3. The elderly woman appeared very fragile.

_____ 4. The farmer grew corn on his 120 acres of land.

_____ 5. Sara is very healthy.

_____ 6. The story seemed odd to us.

_____ 7. The alarm at midnight sounded fearful.

_____ 8. The cheese smelled rotten.

_____ 9. Try to stay warm.

_____ 10. The milk has turned sour.

_____ 11. The nurse turned the patient.

_____ 12. The man looked agitated.

_____ 13. She looked at the picture.

_____ 14. The pillow feels soft.

_____ 15. Lois remains quiet and listless.

_____ 16. The weather became cold last night.

_____ 17. The farmer grows potatoes for a living.

_____ 18. The corn grew tall and sturdy.

_____ 19. Everyone in the room was jubilant.

_____ 20. She looked sleepy in the car.

_____ 21. Despite the rain our fruit trees remained healthy.

_____ 22. The blister grew painful.

_____ 23. The house looked a mess after the party.

_____ 24. Ants are a pest, especially on a picnic day.

_____ 25. The numbers on my calculator appear faint.

Degrees of Adjectives

Many adjectives have three degrees of comparison: **positive, comparative,** and **superlative.**

Positive

This degree is used when only one thing is described.

> This box is heavy.
>
> That sore must be painful.

Comparative

This degree is used when two things are being compared.

> Jim began to work harder on his job.
>
> That is an older piece of luggage.

Superlative

This degree is used when three or more things are being compared.

> This is the hardest work of all.
>
> This is the oldest piece of luggage.

To form the comparative and superlative degrees of adjectives correctly, follow these rules:

1. Add *er* or *est* to the positive form of most one-syllable and some two-syllable adjectives. Double the final consonant, or change the final *y* to *i* where necessary.

Positive	Comparative	Superlative
heavy	heavier	heaviest
strong	stronger	strongest
wet	wetter	wettest

2. Put *more* or *most* before the positive form of some two-syllable adjectives and nearly all adjectives of three more syllables.

generous	more generous	most generous
peaceful	more peaceful	most peaceful
responsible	more responsible	most responsible

3. Memorize these irregular forms of adjectives.

good, well	better	best
bad, ill	worse	worst
far	farther	farthest
far	further	furthest
little	less	least
many	more	most

Exercise 102

Directions: Underline the adjective and write *C* if it is comparative or *S* if it is superlative. Then write its positive form.

Example: This was my <u>worst</u> school year.   *S   bad*

1. John is more congenial than Ted.   _____

2. This is the brightest horse on the market.   _____

3. Jean is happier than Bill.   _____

4. Luke dresses the best.   _____

5. Lucy is the more reliable of the two.   _____

6. She is more attractive in that dress.   _____

7. He is the most obnoxious boy I know.   _____

8. Who is the stronger, Pete or Jim?   _____

9. That car is faster.   _____

10. He was less competent than Keith.   _____

11. In your class, who works the hardest?   _____

12. Mary was the least eager to go.   _____

13. This package is lighter than that one.   _____

14. He was wealthier than Bob.   _____

15. Jenny is the least willing to help.   _____

16. I think Joe's essay is better.   _____

17. His card was the most friendly.   _____

18. This was the best out of ten.   _____

19. The guests arrived earlier than expected.   _____

20. Math is the most difficult test of all.   _____

Directions: Underline the correct answer.

Example: He is the (older, <u>oldest</u>) student in our class.

1. The damage done by tornadoes is (worse, worst) than that done by earthquakes.

2. Of the two girls, Sally is the (brightest, brighter).

3. That was the (best, better) day of my life.

4. Keith is the (more, most) interesting person in the room.

5. She is the (younger, youngest) person to win an Olympic gold medal.

6. Paul is the (more, most) attractive boy in the class.

7. Miss Jones is a (best, better) teacher than her predecessor.

8. Of the two speakers, Bess is the (best, better).

9. This book is the (more, most) suspenseful of the three.

10. Jacqueline is certainly a (best, better) actress than her sister.

11. Paul was the (most, more) courageous of the two.

12. Which major city in Maine is the (further, furthest) from the coast?

13. Becky is the (more, most) energetic girl I know.

14. Jack is by far the (more, most) witty person in the school.

15. Of the two running for office, Bob is the (best, better) qualified.

16. In business, he will probably be the (least, less) successful of his friends.

17. Marilyn is the (happiest, happier) when she is dancing.

18. Our house is the (farther, farthest) one from the corner.

19. This is the (largest, larger) of the two bedrooms.

20. Jane is the (more, most) dependable girl I know.

Directions: Write original sentences that use each of the following words in the degree indicated

1. great (comparative)

2. smooth (superlative)

3. slow (superlative)

4. responsible (comparative)

5. further (comparative)

6. kind (positive)

7. funny (comparative)

8. strict (superlative)

9. lively (superlative)

10. weak (superlative)

Verbs Used as Adjectives

Many verbs are often used as adjectives. Those ending in *ing* and *ed* sometimes are used as adjectives.

> The bell was ringing. (verb)
>
> The ringing bell disturbed his concentration. (adjective)

Exercise 105

Directions: Write *A* if the underlined word is an adjective; *V* if it is a verb or part of the verb.

Example: She won the <u>spelling</u> bee.   *A*

_____ 1.   The children waited in the <u>pouring</u> rain for the bus.

_____ 2.   The <u>melted</u> ice made the walk very slippery.

_____ 3.   I had <u>lost</u> my keys.

_____ 4.   The spectators were <u>cheering</u> loudly.

_____ 5.   Will you please meet us in the <u>waiting</u> room?

_____ 6.   The <u>exhausted</u> child finally fell asleep.

_____ 7.   The <u>cheering</u> crowd almost took the roof off the gym.

_____ 8.   I found my <u>lost</u> keys in the car.

_____ 9.   We finally <u>completed</u> the assignment.

_____ 10.   My <u>completed</u> assignment received an A.

_____ 11.   The <u>frightened</u> child ran into the house.

_____ 12.   We were <u>frightened</u> by the thunder and lightning.

_____ 13. My essay was <u>typed</u> late at night.

_____ 14. We were <u>waiting</u> for the doctor for over an hour.

_____ 15. My <u>typed</u> essay was read by the teacher.

_____ 16. We are taking <u>swimming</u> lessons this summer.

_____ 17. The <u>hurrying</u> waitress spilled the soup.

_____ 18. Her <u>gardening</u> skills are remarkable.

_____ 19. I was <u>hurrying</u> to finish on time.

_____ 20. They were <u>swimming</u> in our pool.

Exercise 106

Directions: Underline the adjectives in the following paragraph. Do not underline articles.

> In August of last year, my friends and I spent a week at the beach. It was a perfect time for our long-awaited vacation. The weather was warm with a cool breeze blowing most of the time. The water was not cold and the waves were perfect for surfing. We played in the water all morning. In the afternoon we lay on the warm sand letting the gentle breeze blow over our warm bodies. We talked about many things for a short time, and then we slept for a couple of hours. After a delicious dinner, we visited the numerous colorful shops filled with every possible type of beach displays. Later in the evening we listened to the raucous music of young, enthusiastic musicians until early morning. After a restful sleep another new day began with more surfing fun and exhilarating adventures.

Exercise 107

Write a paragraph about a perfect place you have visited or one you can imagine. Underline the adjectives you used.

Exercise 108

Replace the trite underlined adjective with an adjective or adjectives that are fresher and more relevant.

Example: My brother bought a <u>neat</u> car yesterday. *My brother bought a four-wheel-drive car yesterday.*

1. My mother had an <u>awful</u> headache all day yesterday.

2. My cousin bought a <u>cute</u> <u>little</u> house.

3. I bought a <u>dandy</u> computer.

4. My friend had a <u>really</u> <u>awful</u> case of hives.

5. We had a <u>nice</u> time.

Unit 6 Review

1. Adjectives describe or modify a noun. The process by which an adjective modifies a word is called *modification*.

2. When you add an adjective to an noun, you immediately limit it. An adjective can describe a noun, state which one, tell how many, or state how much.

3. Articles are classified as adjectives. *The* is a definite article because it refers to a specific person, place, or thing. The articles *a* and *an* are indefinite articles because they refer to any one of a class of persons, places or things. The indefinite pronoun *a* is used before consonant sounds. The indefinite pronoun *an* is used before vowel sounds.

4. Proper adjectives are derived from proper nouns. Proper adjectives must be capitalized.

5. Adjectives are called predicate adjectives when they follow linking verbs and describe the subject.

6. Some verbs can be both action verbs and linking depending on their use. The most common ones are *appear, become, feel, grow, look, sound, taste, remain, smell, stay,* and *turn.* They are linking when they link the subject with the adjective and you can substitute some form of the verb *to be.*

7. Adjectives have three degrees: positive, comparative, and superlative.

    Positive: one thing is described

    Comparative: two things are compared

    Superlative: three or more things are compared.

8. To form comparative and superlative adjectives, add *er* or *est* to the positive form of most one-syllable adjectives and some two-syllable adjectives. Put *more* or *most* or *less* or *least* before the positive form of two-syllable adjectives and nearly all adjectives of three or more syllables.

9. Irregular forms of the adjective should be memorized.

Unit 6
Review Test

Part A.

Directions: Underline the adjectives in the following sentences and put parentheses around the nouns they modify.

1. The concoction was a strange mixture of several strange herbs.

2. He was a poor old farmer who cultivated a run-down apple orchard.

3. This account of the Boston Tea Party is a little bit history and some fiction.

4. Tom was given the second lead in the school play.

5. He had to wear a coarse black wig and a heavy red-lined cape.

6. A fire of pine logs blazed in the stone fireplace.

7. My mother wore a blue velvet dress with an extraordinary long skirt and a black jacket.

8. I was very uncomfortable in that sparse closet-like bedroom.

9. Edison believed that intense brainwork was the real secret of health and longevity.

10. He was always an avid reader of books on a variety of subjects.

Part B.

Directions: Write *C* if the adjective is comparative and *S* if the adjective is superlative.

_____ 1.   It was a longer trip than I anticipated.

_____ 2.   I had less money for Christmas than I expected.

_____ 3.   It was the best debate I had ever heard.

_____ 4.   His house is the farthest on the block.

_____ 5.   Helping her was the least he could do.

_____ 6.   We should have more spectators tomorrow.

_____ 7.   The worst disaster occurred in January.

_____ 8.   I think my sister is feeling better this morning.

_____ 9.   The latest news about the accident will be released tomorrow.

_____ 10.   Tony serves delicious meals but Jane's are better.

Part C.

Directions: Write *L* if the verb is a linking verb and *A* if it is an action verb.

_____ 1.   Terry became anxious when he did not come.

_____ 2.   This banana tastes different.

_____ 3.   We all tasted the cook's samples.

_____ 4. We stayed in that cold cabin all night.

_____ 5. It seemed colder in our room.

_____ 6. At the sound Molly was afraid.

_____ 7. Jennifer grows flowers as a hobby.

_____ 8. He appeared doubtful.

_____ 9. The sound of the bell was pleasant.

_____ 10. The material felt smooth.

_____ 11. The room smelled stuffy.

_____ 12. She remained there for about five minutes.

_____ 13. Mary remained calm throughout the entire ordeal.

_____ 14. Tina looked everywhere for a clue.

_____ 15. Julie became agitated at the video.

Part D.

Directions: Rewrite the proper adjectives with correct capitalization.

1. The korean people have many wonderful customs.

2. Could you make me a xerox copy?

3. They were french-speaking immigrants.

4. They refused to attend a anti-nazi rally.

5. We met a lovely indian woman in a sari.

6. The franklin d. roosevelt years were sometimes difficult for America.

7. The band directed by major leonard played some rousing marching music.

8. They greeted the president of the united states.

9. Did you meet ex-senator longren?

10. The african-american groups held rallies.

11. People seem to enjoy paris fashions.

12. I think arabic is very difficult.

13. Did you ever go to the kentucky derby?

14. In ancient mythology the goddess athena dispensed wisdom.

15. We traveled on the trans-world airlines.

Unit 7
Adverbs

What Is an Adverb?

An **adverb** is a word that modifies a verb, an adjective or another adverb. Adverbs, like adjectives, are modifiers. They slightly change the meaning of other words by making them more specific.

Adverbs Modify Verbs

Adverbs modify verbs by answering any of five questions: Where? When? Why? In what manner? (How?) and To what extent?

Where

> The students stood and saluted the nearby flag.
> The car passed slowly by.

When

> He will visit us later.
> I must leave now.

How

> Dave did his work quickly.
> She looked around the room eagerly.

To What Extent

> Marcia did her work completely.
> She did her work partially.

Exercise 109

Directions: Underline the adverbs in the following sentences.

Example: We will return <u>soon</u>.

1. I plan to give you my outline immediately.

2. She went about her work quietly.

3. Jim arrived at the party late.

4. John spoke rapidly.

5. She had scarcely any chance to reply.

6. Mike drove his new car carefully.

7. My friend Jon is moving away.

8. She courageously faced the problem.

9. Is your sister fully recovered from the accident?

10. We approached the cage cautiously.

11. Are you going to Canada today?

12. The plane arrived early.

13. The meeting ended abruptly.

14. She only partially understood the question.

15. I did not want to go to the dance.

16. I never made that remark.

17. She did her work hastily.

18. Be sure to wash yourself completely.

19. The baseball unexpectedly broke a window.

20. You should have spoken before.

Adverbs modify adjectives by answering one question: To what extent?

My brother was unusually quiet this morning.

Unusually is an adverb modifying the adjective *quiet.*

Exercise 110

Directions: Underline the adjective and write the adverb that modifies it.

Example: I was extremely <u>angry</u> when I heard the news. *extremely*

1. His sister is highly intelligent. _____

2. Your answer is partially correct. _____

3. I was very happy to see my cousin. _____

4. The hike made me overly tired. _____

5. The bus was almost full of rowdy youngsters. _____

6. The road ahead was barely visible in the storm. _____

7. We were somewhat annoyed at his actions. _____

8. It was an unusual piercing cry. _____

9. The street lights were hardly bright enough
    to help us see our way home. _____

10. Ted was extremely overjoyed at winning first place. _____

11. We became completely bored with the lecture. _____

12. My little sister is very tall for her age. _____

13. I was definitely overjoyed at my promotion. _____

14. He was completely disappointed at the
    results of his final exam.   _____

15. She was never sad at the outcome.   _____

16. The light made Ted partially blind.   _____

17. Becky was somewhat satisfied after his apology. _____

18. Al is frequently tardy for school.   _____

19. TV today is too violent.   _____

20. Sara was extremely depressed for no good reason. _____

Adverbs can modify another adverb. The adverb comes directly before the
adverb it modifies.

Exercise 111

Directions: Underline the adverb and write the adverb that modifies it.

Example: She left extremely <u>quickly</u>. *extremely*

1. Tom awoke very early on Saturday morning.   _____

2. The mud slides in Italy occurred very suddenly. _____

3. The teacher came unusually late for class.   _____

4. Jane answered his question somewhat slowly.   _____

5. The cookies were almost completely eaten.   _____

6. Bob responded to the allegations too hastily.   _____

7. We cannot leave the classroom too soon.   _____

8. Sally worked extremely hard on her science project. _____

9. You cannot handle that material too carefully. _____

10. Joyce spoke more intelligently than her friend. _____

11. He always does his assignments very thoroughly. _____

12. He worked rather quietly all morning.   _____

13. You should act more quickly in an emergency.   _____

14. He was quite definitely sure of his answers. _____

15. We will be leaving for the movies very soon. _____

16. Many poor people need much more food. _____

17. She looked rather sternly at the boy's actions. _____

18. He talked very convincingly to the judge. _____

19. My friend worked very quickly. _____

20. He responded somewhat slower than his brother. _____

Exercise 112

Directions: Complete the following sentences by adding the suggested adverbs.

Example: My uncle is a skilled technician. (adverb modifying adjective)
My uncle is a highly skilled technician.

1. The pilot landed the airplane. (how)

2. Running the bases during a game, I stopped suddenly. (adverb modifying adverb)

3. Josh became angry. (adverb modifying adjective)

4. She finished her job and went. (where)

5. Judy is driving. (how)

6. Jim loves a fast boat. (adverb modifying adjective)

7. The rocket show was held. (where)

8. Jane walked rapidly to the store. (adverb modifying adverb)

9. Suzie won the race. (how)

10. The hostess was polite. (adverb modifying adjective)

Adverbs vs. Adjectives

Adjectives modify nouns and pronouns.

> beautiful smile   inspiring talk
>
> rapid river   red-eyed monster

Adverbs modify verbs, adjectives, and other adverbs.

> walked slowly   how
>
> came late   when
>
> extremely happy   adverb, adjective
>
> very slowly   adverb, adverb

Exercise 113

Directions: If the underlined word is an adverb, write *ADV*. If it is an adjective, write *ADJ*.

Example: We walked through the park <u>slowly</u>.   *ADV*

_____ 1. The spectators cheered <u>enthusiastically</u>.

_____ 2. Jeff's talk was <u>unusually</u> short.

_____ 3. We saw a <u>great</u> movie last night.

_____ 4. Friday was a <u>long</u> day.

_____ 5. He had a <u>close</u> call on the freeway.

_____ 6. Everyone waited <u>eagerly</u> for the announcement.

_____ 7. My friend lives <u>close</u> to school.

_____ 8. Ted is always an <u>eager</u> student.

_____ 9. Joan gave me a little <u>sisterly</u> warning.

_____ 10. The officer responded <u>quickly</u> to our call.

_____ 11. <u>Last</u> month has been busy.

_____ 12. A Mercury just drove <u>past</u>.

_____ 13. Jean was <u>extremely</u> unhappy over her grades.

_____ 14. The officer <u>openly</u> admitted his mistake.

_____ 15. We enjoyed the concert <u>immensely</u>.

_____ 16. The curtains were blowing in the <u>gentle</u> breeze.

_____ 17. We generally walk <u>leisurely</u> to school each morning.

_____ 18. The judge's response was <u>very</u> fair.

_____ 19. We <u>thoroughly</u> enjoyed the picnic.

_____ 20. The weather yesterday was <u>unusually</u> sunny.

Exercise 114

Directions: Add adverbs to the following sentences.

Example: Helen Keller's life is *truly* inspiring.

1. When Helen was only eighteen months old, an illness _____ destroyed both her sight and hearing.

2. She lived in a silent, dark world, yelling_____ when she wanted anything.

3. Mr. Keller _____ hired Annie Sullivan to teach Helen.

4. After days of frustrating endeavors, Annie _____ established contact with Helen.

5. She _____ spelled words on Helen's hand with her fingers.

6. One day, with the word *water* and feeling water at the same time, Helen _____saw the connection between the words spelled on her hand and their meaning.

7. She _____ learned to speak.

8. Helen's progress was _____ rapid.

9. She _____ earned a degree from Radcliffe College.

10. She was _____ grateful to Annie Sullivan for helping her out of her intellectual darkness.

11. She was able to give _____speeches to enraptured audiences.

12. She also worked _____ to help other blind and deaf children.

Degrees of Comparison

Like adjectives, adverbs have three degrees of comparison: positive, comparative, and superlative. The degrees are practically the same in both adjectives and adverbs. The comparative degree always compares two; the superlative degree always compares three or more.

Positive	Comparative	Superlative
late	later	latest
well	better	best

Note
All adverbs that end with the suffix *ly*, regardless of the number of syllables, form their comparative and superlative degrees with *more, most* or *less, least.*

smoothly	more smoothly	most smoothly
quickly	less quickly	least quickly

Directions: Write the correct form of the adjective or adverb to complete the sentence.

Example: We tried *harder* than our friends did. (hard)

1. Sally is _____ than her sister. (smart)

2. She is the _____ girl in her class. (intelligent)

3. This water is _____ now than it was yesterday. (clear)

4. He crept _____ into his room. (silent)

5. Our new car is _____ than our last car. (sturdy)

6. He worked _____ doing work on that old building. (cautious)

7. Dave is the _____ boy in our class. (witty)

8. In danger, Jerry acts _____ than I do. (fearless)

9. Kathy has _____ than any other girl in her class. (initiative)

10. In the race, Leon came the _____. (close)

Directions: Write the appropriate form of the modifier to make the sentence correct.

Example: Our cat is pretty, but your cat is the *prettiest* pet on the block.

1. John is happy, but Marilyn is the _____ of all the students.

2. My mother was ill but today she is _____ . (well)

3. This is certainly the _____ of the two stories. (good)

4. John's house is _____ away than Ted's house. (far)

5. Cynthia was late for class, but Tommy was _____ .

6. Barbara has less money than I, but Jan has the _____ money of all.

7. His sister often acts childish, but my sister acts even _____ .

8. That package is heavy, but this one is _____ .

9. She works quickly, but he works _____ .

10. The situation was the _____ hopeless of any I have ever encountered.

11. Jean is the _____ popular girl in the school.

12. Of the two athletes, Jan is the _____ .(good)

13. It is warm in the room, but you will be _____ by the fire.

14. Often the book is _____ interesting than the movie.

15. This car drives _____ smoothly than the last one I had.

16. Our parlor is the _____
    room in the house. (large)

17. Paul is short, but Tim is the _____ boy on the team.

18. I was sad at his death, but his sister was _____ .

19. Today is sunny, but Tuesday was the _____ day of the entire week.

20. His singing was good, but Geraldine's was much _____ .

*Problems with
Adverbs and
Adjectives*

Bad/Badly and Good/Well

Bad is an adjective, not an adverb. It should never be used after an action verb.

> He works bad. (incorrect)
> Junior played bad. (incorrect)

Bad can be used as an adjective only after a linking verb.

> Jean felt bad about the accident.

Badly is an adverb. It follows an action verb.

> I played badly.

It can never be used as an adjective after a linking verb.

> She felt badly. (incorrect)

Good is an adjective. It must modify a noun.

> That was a good show.

Well is generally an adverb.

> He played the piano well.

Note
When *well* is used to mean "healthy," it is an adjective and can be used after a linking verb.

> John felt well this morning.
> My sister is well today.
> After a long illness, Dave is now well.

Real/Really and Sure/Surely

Really and *surely* are adverbs and should modify verbs, adjectives, and other adverbs.

Verbs	My mother surely cares for her children.
Adverbs	Her car is really fast.
Adjectives	That record is really hot.

Real and *sure* are adjectives and should modify nouns.

Noun	It was a real diamond.
	My horse was a sure winner.

Exercise 117

Directions: Underline the correct form.

Example: He is always so (<u>sure</u>, surely) of himself.

1. Which of the twins is the (more, most) intelligent?

2. He is certainly the (more, most) talented actor on TV.

3. Her baby was the (most, more) beautiful child I have ever seen.

4. In class, Jerry is (less, least) willing to cooperate than Frank.

5. Of the members of my class, Sally has the (more, most) complete notes.

6. My brother is (smarter, smartest) than I.

7. She was (real, really) happy at the results of the test.

8. Julie played (bad, badly) in the concert.

9. He doesn't feel (well, good) this morning.

10. Gerald felt (bad, badly) when he heard about the tragedy.

11. Margie plays the violin (good, well).

12. The rehearsal went (well, good) today.

13. He is (sure, surely) aware of the consequences.

14. It did not (real, really) matter to her.

15. That is a (really, real) piece of evidence.

16. Maria is (sure, surely) kind.

17. Jane danced very (good, well) in the contest.

18. Jack was (more, most) nervous than he was yesterday.

19. Jim's condition is even (worse, worser) than I thought.

20. It was (real, really) no concern of mine.

21. Jill is not only pretty, she is the (prettier, prettiest) in the town.

22. If you want to do (well, good) you must practice more.

23. This fire feels (good, well) on a cold, winter night.

24. At summer camp, we always eat (good, well).

25. That oven is (real, really) hot.

Exercise 118

Directions: On addtional paper, write original sentences using the following words correctly.

1. the superlative of *quick*
2. the comparative of *slow*
3. the positive of *good*
4. the comparative of *fine*
5. the positive of *well*

6. the superlative of *late*
7. the comparative of *difficult*
8. the superlative of *slow*
9. the positive of *bad*
10. the superlative of *good*

Double Negatives

A common mistake with modifiers is using more than one negative. The most common way to make a statement negative is to use only one negative word. Negative words are *never, no, nobody, none, not, nothing,* and *nowhere.* The contraction *n't* also makes a sentence negative.

More than one negative in a sentence implies positive.

> I hadn't had nothing to eat all day.

This sentence implies that you have had something. If you didn't have nothing, you must have had something.

When *but* means "only," it generally acts as a negative.

> *There wasn't but none left* means *There was none left.*

Other negative words are *barely, hardly,* or *scarcely.*

We didn't scarcely know him.	*We scarcely knew him.*
I couldn't hardly see in the storm.	*I could hardly see the storm.*
She wasn't barely in the room when it happened.	*She was barely in the room when it happened.*

Exercise 119

Directions: Underline the word that makes the sentence correct.

Example: Haven't you (never, <u>ever</u>) heard of this person?

1. Carol said she doesn't want (anything, nothing) today.

2. She couldn't believe that I had done (nothing, anything) wrong.

3. Sue (hadn't, had) barely left her porch.

4. There weren't (any, no) stop signs at that corner.

5. Don't they (never, ever) slow down on that street?

6. She scarcely (ever, never) crosses the street at that corner.

7. She didn't say (nothing, anything) about the award.

8. Clara didn't write (no, any) complaining letter.

9. Miss Jones didn't excuse (no one, anyone) from taking the test.

10. I don't (never, ever) want to hear that expression again.

11. I couldn't talk to (no one, anyone) about the problem.

12. She wouldn't agree to discuss it with (no one, anyone).

13. This little town doesn't have (no, any) street lights.

14. She didn't realize that (anyone, no one) was there.

15. Jean couldn't be going (anywhere, nowhere) soon.

Unit 7 Review

1. An adverb is a word that modifies a verb, an adjective, or another adverb.

2. Adverbs modify verbs by asking the questions *where, when, why, how,* and *to what extent.*

3. Adverbs have three degrees of comparison: positive, comparative, and superlative. They form degrees the same way adjectives form degrees. The one exception is that all adverbs ending in *ly* form the comparative and superlative degrees with *more, most* or *less, least.*

4. a. *Bad* is an adjective, not an adverb. It can be used as an adjective after a linking verb.

   b. *Badly* is an adverb.

   c. *Good* is an adjective.

   d. *Well* is generally an adverb. When *well* is used to mean "healthy," it is an adjective and can be used after linking verbs.

   e. *Really* and *surely* are adverbs. *Real* and *sure* are adjectives.

5. When using modifiers, avoid using more than one negative in a sentence.

Unit 7
Review Test

Part A.

Directions: Underline the adverbs in the following sentences.

1. Jenny played the trumpet well.

2. Susanna always speaks softly in the classroom.

3. Bob barely passed his math test.

4. Several of the students plan to go later.

5. She could hardly see him in the dark.

6. Jeff shouted loudly and angrily.

7. Sara looked around cautiously.

8. My father was somewhat displeased with my grade in math.

9. The club finally adopted its constitution.

10. Her little brother rarely talks.

11. I am going to do my homework soon.

12. My friend lives nearby.

13. The construction company was completely late in finishing our house.

14. It was too late to go to the library.

15. We left the book inside.

16. The man saw the girl once in the past week.

17. Our librarian always works systematically.

18. We finally agreed on something.

19. Richard usually goes to the gym each morning.

20. We found the paper partially hidden in a box.

Part B.

Directions: Write *ADV* if the underlined word is an adverb. Write *ADJ* if it is an adjective.

_____ 1. Our teacher is <u>strict</u>.

_____ 2. She is <u>surely</u> willing to help us.

_____ 3. Dan plays the piano <u>well</u>.

_____ 4. A <u>good</u> time was had by all of us.

_____ 5. Jane is <u>sure</u> to know the results of the vote.

_____ 6. We were <u>really</u> tired after our hike.

_____ 7. Mike laughed <u>easily</u> at the joke.

_____ 8. We took a <u>leisurely</u> walk to the beach.

_____ 9. *Titanic* is an <u>outstanding</u> movie.

_____ 10. Do you live <u>close</u> to Disneyland?

Part C.

Directions: Write *P* if the positive form is used, *C* if the comparative form is used, or *S* if the superlative form is used.

_____ 1. Do you think he writes well?

_____ 2. She is better in math.

_____ 3. Of the two, Beth is the better.

_____ 4. She is the least responsible of the children.

_____ 5. Her answers are generally complete.

_____ 6. Tom is the best athlete in the school.

_____ 7. Jean's French is the most fluent.

_____ 8. In the class, who is the most diligent?

_____ 9. Lincoln was greater than any other U.S. President.

_____ 10. Jenny's grades are higher than Jim's.

Part D.

Directions: Underline the word that makes the sentence correct.

1. Jean sings (good, well).

2. He is (surely, sure) to achieve success.

3. Was Elena (really, real) concerned about Bob?

4. Art didn't have (anything, nothing) of which to accuse her.

5. Caroline's hair style is (more, most) stylish than Joan's.

6. Who is the (stronger, strongest) in your family?

7. That restaurant is the (closer, closest) of any in the city.

8. Steve is surely (more, most) intelligent than Peter.

9. Who is the (more, most) lively of the two sisters?

10. Larry is the (more, most) handsome TV star.

Unit 8
Conjunctions and Interjections

What Is a Conjunction?

A **conjunction** is a word that joins words or groups of words. It connects similar kinds of words that are grammatically alike.

The conjunctions we will study are the coordinating conjunctions. They are *and, but, or, nor, for, so,* and *yet.* These words can be used to join

a. *Nouns and Pronouns*

> Julie and I are good friends.
> The teacher and her class held a day for the poor.

b. *Verbs*

> Bob worked hard all day yet enjoyed himself in the evening.

c. *Adjectives*

> Jane was arrogant and proud.

d. *Adverbs*

> Jon walked quickly but cautiously.

e. *Prepositional phrases*

> She put the groceries in the refrigerator and the other items on the shelf.

Exercise 120

Directions: Underline the conjunctions in the following sentences.

Example: I made some tomato soup <u>and</u> a grilled cheese sandwich.

1. Joel ate his lunch and went to the game.

2. She sat by the fire alone but not unhappy.

3. You can read the news in the newspaper or listen to it on TV.

4. John brought his guitar and banjo to school.

5. The little puppy could not see, nor could he feed himself.

6. She wore a simple yet stylish dress.

7. Enter here or at the back of the park.

8. I listened to the news and reported it immediately.

9. You can interview him here or at his home.

10. Please give me a hot dog or a hamburger.

Directions: Use the following prompts to write original sentences on another piece of paper.

1. Join two adjectives with *or.*
2. Join two verbs with *and.*
3. Join two linking verbs with *but.*
4. Join two adverbs with *and.*
5. Join two pronouns with *or.*
6. Join two imperative sentences with *or.*
7. Join two subjects with *and.*
8. Join two prepositional phrases with *or.*
9. Join two verbs with *or*
10. Join two pronouns with *and.*

What Is an Interjection?

An **interjection** is an exclamatory word that expresses strong emotion. It does not have a grammatical relation with the rest of the sentence. It is separated with an exclamation mark.

Interjections can express a variety of emotions. Note how interjections are punctuated.

Ouch! That really hurts!   Wait! I need your help!
Whew! That was a close call!   Oh! What a disaster!

Some common interjections

ah	gee	goodness	gosh
help	hey	hurray	oh
oops	ouch	psst	whew

Exercise 122

Directions: Add interjections to the following sentences.

Example: *Hey!* Watch out for that car!

1. _____ I dropped all the eggs!
2. _____ I cut my finger!
3. _____ What a great game!
4. _____ It's worse than I thought!
5. _____ It's hot!
6. _____ I dropped grease on my best blouse!
7. _____ I'm falling!
8. _____ I shouted!
9. _____ What a great night!
10. _____ It's too late now!
11. _____ What am I going to do!
12. _____ Dial 911!

13. _____ It's an earthquake!

14. _____ It's a home run!

15. _____ You better fake it!

16. _____ Come here!

17. _____ That's not the way to do it!

18. _____ It's a tragedy!

19. _____ Look where you're going!

20. _____ What shall we do!

Exercise 123

Parts of Speech Summary

Directions: Write five original sentences that use interjections.

From your past study of the parts of speech, you know that words are used in many different ways. You should watch the use of a word in a sentence, for the way the word is used determines what part of speech it is.

She likes the color *red.*	noun
She wore a *red* dress.	adjective
There was a terrible *storm* last night.	noun
The soldiers will *storm* the building.	verb
Keep your toys *inside.*	adverb
She walked *inside* the room.	preposition
The *inside* of this box needs repair.	noun

Points to Remember

Nouns and Pronouns

> Subject of a sentence
> Subject following linking verb

Direct and indirect objects

> Objects of a preposition
> These are always nouns or pronouns

Verbs

> Show action or state-of being
> Predicates of a sentence

Prepositions

> Show the relationship between two nouns

Adjectives

> Modify a noun or pronoun
> Predicate adjective

Adverbs

> Modify a verb, adjective, or another adverb

Conjunctions

> Joins words or groups of words

Part of Speech	Definition	Use
Noun	Names a person, place, thing, or idea.	Paul gave Jack his baseball. *subject* *indirect object* *direct object* Mary, my friend, is captain. *subject* *apposition to subject* *linking verb*
Pronoun	Takes the place of a noun or refers to a noun.	She saw him at the mall. *subject* *direct object* *object of preposition* It was she. *subject* *linking verb* *subject*
Verb	Shows action, makes a statement.	Dave saved his money. *action* Pete will be an accountant *linking* Bob ate his lunch. (*active*) Lunch was eaten. (*passive*)
Preposition	Shows relationship between two nouns or pronouns.	(Jill) walked into the (store.) (We) walked behind (him.)
Adjective	Modifies a noun or pronoun.	Her favorite color is red. *adjective* *predicate adjective*
Adverb	Modifies a verb, adjective, or another adverb.	Jane walked quickly. Jane walked very quickly. Jane is very quick.
Conjunction	Joins words or groups of words.	Mary and Jane left early. John or Pete will preside.
Interjection	Shows strong feeling.	Ouch! It hurts!

These words are frequently misunderstood or used incorrectly in speaking and writing. Study these words and work the exercises until you have mastered the entire list.

Accept, Except

Accept, a verb, means "to receive."

I accept your apology.

Except, a preposition, means "leaving out" or "other than."

All left the room except Ray.

Accuse, Allege

Accuse means "to blame" or "to charge someone with a wrongdoing."

She accused me of cheating.

Allege means to claim something that needs to be proved.

The girl alleged that the man held her up and took her wallet.

Adapt, Adopt

Adapt means "to change."

She can easily adapt to the climate.

Adopt means "to take on as one's own."

My mother is going to adopt a new baby.

Advice, Advise

Advice, a noun, means "an opinion."

Her advice to me was to stop smoking.

Advise, a verb means "to give an opinion."

I advise you to give up smoking.

Affect, Effect

Affect is usually a verb meaning "to influence" or "to bring about a change in."

Her death affected me greatly.

Effect is usually a noun and means "result."

One effect of that medicine is dizziness.

Aggravate, Irritate

Aggravate means "to make worse."

Sitting on the cement steps will only aggravate your cold.

Irritate means "to annoy."

Your actions irritate me.

All ready, Already

All ready, an adjective, means "ready."

The eighth grade is all ready to take the bus.

Already, an adverb, means "to or before this time."

The class is already on the bus.

All right, Alright

Always use *all right* in your writing. *Alright* is not considered correct.

It is all right for you to leave now.

All together, Altogether	*All together,* an adverb, means "all at once," or together as a group.
	The class sang all together.
	Altogether, an adverb, means "completely," or "in all."
	There is altogether too much mischief brewing.
Allusion, Illusion	An *allusion* is a reference to something.
	Her allusions to Greek mythology are often incorrect.
	An *illusion* is a mistaken idea.
	He had great illusions of grandeur.
A lot, Alot, Allot	*A lot* is an informal expression that means "a great many" or a "large amount." It is never written as one word.
	She had a lot of nerve coming here.
	Allot means "to divide in parts" or to "give out in shares."
	My grandfather will allot each of us enough money for college.
Amount, Number	*Amount* refers to a singular word.
	A large amount of money is in his room.
	Number always refers to a plural verb.
	A large number of coins were in the drawer.
	The number refers to a singular verb.
	The number of days is ten.
Among, Between	*Among* and *between* are prepositions.
	Among always implies three or more.
	Divide the papers among the class.
	Between implies two.
	Divide the papers between Jane and Irene.
Anxious	*Anxious* means "worry." Never use *anxious* for *eager.*
	She was anxious about the outcome of the trial.
	She was eager to hear the news.
Anyone, Everyone, Any one, Every one	*Anyone* and *everyone* mean "any person" or "every person," respectively. They are used as pronouns.
	Everyone in the room has musical talent.
	Anyone can help us decorate.
	Any one means "any singular person or thing."
	Every one means "every single person or thing."
	Any one of these problems is possible.
	Every one of these colors is appropriate.

At	Never use *at* after *where*. Just eliminate it.
	Where do I catch the bus at?
	Where do I catch the bus?
A While, Awhile	*A while* is an article and a noun and is usually used after the preposition *for.*
	We waited for a while and then left.
	Awhile is an adverb which means "for a while."
	Please stand here awhile.
Beside, Besides	These prepositions have different meanings and cannot be interchanged. *Beside* means "at the side of," or "close to."
	She sat beside her parents.
	Besides means "in addition to."
	Who is going to the movie besides me?
Bring, Take	*Bring* means "to carry from a distant place to a nearer one."
	Please bring that book from the library to me.
	Take means "to carry from a near place to a more distant one."
	Please take this box to the post office.
Different from, Different than	It is better to use *different from.*
	She is much different from the rest of us.
Don't, Doesn't	Use *doesn't* with all third person singular pronouns and nouns.
	She doesn't wish to go.
	I don't want to go to the concert.
Emigrate, Immigrate	*Emigrate* means "to leave a country."
	They emigrated from Russia.
	Immigrate means "to enter a country."
	My parents immigrated from Italy.
Enthusiastic, Enthused	*Enthusiastic* is the acceptable form. Avoid using *enthused.*
	The cheerleaders were very enthusiastic.
Further, Farther	*Farther* refers to distance.
	She lives farther from me.
	Further means "additional."
	There was nothing further on the agenda.
Fewer, Less	Use *fewer* with things that can be counted.
	Use fewer eggs in that cake.
	Use *less* with things that cannot be counted.
	She had less light than she needed.

Former, Latter	*Former* refers to the first of previously mentioned items.
	The former of the two essays is the better.
	Latter refers to the second of the two.
	The latter essay was not submitted for the contest.
Healthy, Healthful	People are *healthy*. Things are *healthful*.
	Jeff is very healthy.
	This food is healthful.
In, Into	*In* always refers to position.
	Her hand is in the bag.
	Into refers to motion.
	She walked into the room.
Irregardless, Regardless	Do not use *irregardless*. Use *regardless* instead.
	Regardless of your opinion, I am going to submit the article.
Learn, Teach	*Learn* means "to acquire knowledge."
	We learned how to measure distance.
	Teach means "to give knowledge."
	My mother taught me how to sew.
Leave, Let	*Leave* means "to allow to remain."
	Please leave that box on the table.
	Let means "to permit."
	Let me teach the lesson tomorrow.
Lose, Loose	*Lose,* a verb, means "to miss from one's possessions."
	You will lose your wallet if you're not careful.
	Loose is generally an adjective.
	That screw is loose.
May be, Maybe	*May* is a helping verb; *be* is a verb.
	She may be able to teach for you tomorrow.
	Maybe, an adverb, means "perhaps."
	Maybe we will go with you tomorrow.
Outside of	Do not use this expression to mean *besides* or *except*.
	Outside of my brothers, no one pitched in to help. (incorrect)
	Except for my brothers, no one pitched in to help.
Ought	Never use ought with *have* or *had*. Eliminate *have* or *had*.
	I really ought to phone my mother now.

Plenty	*Plenty* is a noun that is usually correctly followed by *of,* as in *plenty of room.* It does not mean "very."
	There was plenty of food for the picnic.
Precede, Proceed	*Precede* means "to go before."
	Joan will precede you in the contest.
	Proceed means "to move or go forward."
	She will now proceed to give us her opinion.
Principal, Principle	*Principal* is an adjective. It means "head" or "chief."
	Mr. Jones is an excellent principal.
	The principal cause of the accident is not known.
	Principle is a noun. It means "a truth or law."
	She always acts on principle.
Raise, Rise	The verb *raise* always takes an object and means "to lift," "to increase" or "to grow."
	They always raise a good crop of corn.
	I cannot raise this window.
	Rise never takes an object. It means "to move upward" or "to be increased."
	Please rise when the principal enters.
Real	*Real* means "authentic." Do not use in place of *very* or *really.*
	It is a real antique.
Set, Sit	*Set* takes an object and means "to put."
	Please set that vase of flowers on the table.
	Sit never takes an object. It means "to be seated."
	Please sit in the third row.
Stationary, Stationery	*Stationary* means "not moving."
	The bench was stationary.
	Stationery means "writing paper."
	She wrote a letter on pink stationery.
Than, Then	*Than* is used in comparisons.
	He is happier than I.
	Then, an adverb, refers to time.
	Then they left.

Their, There, They're	*Their* is a possessive pronoun.
	It was their decision.
	There is an adverb.
	They worked there for years.
	They're is a contraction for they are.
	They're leaving tomorrow.
To, Too, Two	*To* is a preposition.
	Everyone walked to town.
	Too is an adverb and modifies adjectives or other adverbs.
	The statement was too absurd.
	Two is a number.
	There were two boys in the room.
Unique	*Unique* means "one of a kind." Do not use it to mean "odd." Never use "most unique" or "more unique."
Way, Ways	Do not use *ways* (plural) after the article *a*.
	You still have a long ways to drive to work. (incorrect)
	You still have a long way to drive to work.

Exercise 124

Directions: Underline the choice that makes the sentence correct.

Example: We (<u>may be</u>, maybe) allowed to leave early tomorrow.

1. During the summer we liked to stand (besides, beside) the tree.

2. My new teacher is different (than, from) my last one.

3. We planned to go (altogether, all together) in one car.

4. The counselor tried to (advice, advise) him properly.

5. The school (adopted, adapted) a new reading program.

6. (Beside, Besides) a severe cold, Sam had a fever.

7. Please (bring, take) that book to me.

8. We all wanted to go to the beach (accept, except) my father.

9. (Everyone, Every one) visited the museum.

10. The teacher divided the papers (among, between) Mary and me.

11. His goal to be principal was an (allusion, illusion).

12. Despite the storm, everything turned out (all right, alright).

13. We all had to wait for (a while, awhile) for her appearance.

14. I was (eager, anxious) to find out if my absence would be excused.

15. Jane jogged (a while, awhile) before dark.

16. Bob refuses to (except, accept) his inability to be a basketball player.

17. What (stationery, stationary) will you use to write the letter?

18. Does anyone know where the light switch (is, is at)?

19. A hammock was strung (among, between) the two trees.

20. The way you dress is (all together, altogether) inappropriate.

21. The number of weeks left in the school year (is, are) two.

22. The amount of light (was, were) minimal.

23. How did his actions (effect, affect) you?

24. A number of your papers (was, were) corrected yesterday.

25. The (affects, effects) of the long strike were felt everywhere.

Exercise 125

Directions: Underline the word that makes the sentence correct.

Example: The sculpture is (most unique, <u>unique</u>).

1. Do not (aggravate, irritate) me this morning.

2. Cindy has (all ready, already) prepared her acceptance speech.

3. Jean sat (among, between) the boys in her class.

4. The robber took (a lot, allot) of money from the bank.

5. (Anyone, Any one) can try out for the play.

6. Do not be (anxious, eager) to join the drill team.

7. (Everyone, Every one) of the mice was used in the experiment.

8. Would you mind lending me that book for (awhile, a while)?

9. The will of my father will (allot, a lot) each of us $10,000.

10. Did she (emigrate, immigrate) into the United States last year?

11. You need (less, fewer) time on this exercise.

12. The key was found (among, between) all the papers on my desk.

13. Did you know that spinach is (healthy, healthful)?

14. Becky is generally (enthused, enthusiastic) in class.

15. She will (bring, take) her lunch to school.

16. My little sister is certainly different (than, from) me.

17. Will she (immigrate, emigrate) from the Ukraine?

18. (Leave, Let) that material on the table.

19. I (may be, maybe) able to help you later today.

20. The (principal, principle) rule to follow is to love your neighbor.

21. The team was (already, all ready) to leave.

22. The man will (allot, a lot) his son the necessary funds for the trip.

23. The (number, amount) of food wasted is tragic.

24. Marian (doesn't, don't) earn a full salary.

25. (Irregardless, Regardless) of what he says, I am applying there now.

Exercise 126

Directions: Underline the word that makes the sentence correct.

Example: (To, Too, <u>Two</u>) people walked away from the store.

1. Please (rise, raise) your hands before speaking.

2. She could not even (raise, rise) from her chair.

3. (Let, Leave) that material alone.

4. Didn't she (learn, teach) you anything?

5. (Regardless, Irregardless) of the outcome, I cannot stay.

6. She walked (in, into) the room.

7. The steering wheel of her car seems (lose, loose).

8. She put her hand (in, into) the bird's cage.

9. The advertisement had an (illusion, allusion) to Hercules.

10. She (had ought, ought) to leave well enough alone.

11. The (principle, principal) on which she acts is honesty.

12. (They're, Their) leaving soon.

13. That painting by Carol is (unique, most unique).

14. It is (to, too) late to join the choir.

15. Marilyn is heavier (then, than) I.

16. Please (sit, set) the table for me.

17. You can (precede, proceed) with the business meeting now.

18. That item should (proceed, precede) the last one.

19. Would you (let, leave) me go to the mall?

20. All her painting materials were (in, into) her desk at school.

21. In her speech she made (illusions, allusions) to the Bible.

22. How did that defeat (effect, affect) the team?

23. Sally loves to use colored (stationery, stationary).

24. Pat made (less, fewer) mistakes on his paper than Ted.

25. The decision to work was (theirs, there's).

Directions: Underline the word that makes the sentence correct.

Example: (<u>Leave</u>, Let) the dog alone.

1. I have (less, fewer) albums of Frank Sinatra than I want.

2. How did you (advise, advice) her?

3. Did she (accuse, allege) you of any wrongdoing?

4. Jack could not (adopt, adapt) to the change of weather.

5. Running in that weather can (irritate, aggravate) your cough.

6. We were (all ready, already) prepared for the exam.

7. That is (altogether, all together) too much money.

8. There was nothing (farther, further) he could say.

9. (Bring, Take) Jennie to the doctor.

10. My parents (emigrated, immigrated) to the United States in 1940.

11. He (emigrated, immigrated) from Cuba.

12. (Any one, Anyone) of you may choose your own topic.

13. His report was more amusing (than, then) practical.

14. We live a long (way, ways) from the city.

15. She (don't, doesn't) want any special consideration.

16. For (a while, awhile) we sat and listened to the music.

17. She doesn't seem to know where (she's at, she is).

18. We left the grounds after (a while, awhile).

19. My sister (brought, took) me a present from Thailand.

20. Jane, my cousin, is visiting with us for (a while, awhile).

21. To give you (farther, further) assurance, meet me at 9:00 A.M.

22. She makes (less, fewer) mistakes on her computer now.

23. (Any one, Anyone) in this room can help with the cleaning.

24. (Bring, Take) this letter to your mother.

25. Please (sit, set) there.

Directions: Underline the word that makes the sentence correct.

Example: The sandwiches were divided (<u>among</u>, between) the boys.

1. The class was (all together, altogether) too loud.

2. Jim seemed bent on (aggravating, irritating) the teacher this morning.

3. Please stand (stationary, stationery) for two minutes.

4.   Do not (accuse, allege) me of damaging your car.

5.   It is certainly not (all right, alright) to leave now.

6.   Try to use (less, fewer) shortening in your biscuits.

7.   If you (except, accept) my proposition, we will start immediately.

8.   Can we now (precede, proceed) with the interview?

9.   Carol was (to, two, too) unhappy to speak about it.

10. The (affects, effects) of his remarks made her very unhappy.

11. The class was (already, all ready) to go to Disneyland.

12. Does Ray live (further, farther) from school than you?

13. This material is different (than, from) the last batch.

14. (Take, Bring) that report to me.

15. (Beside, Besides) Sally, who else is involved?

16. (Everyone, Every one) of these papers has errors.

17. She enjoys movies (a lot, allot).

18. If you eat well and exercise daily, you should be (healthy, healthful).

19. My father divided the money (between, among) Jeff, Pete and me.

20. Martin (adapted, adopted) the machine for a particular job.

21. We are going to (adapt, adopt) a new plan for our organization.

22. (Any one, Anyone) will be welcome to help us prepare for the dance.

23. We will stay here for (awhile, a while).

24. She was (anxious, eager) to learn about a summer job.

25. What (stationary, stationery) did you use for your invitations?

Exercise 129

Directions: Underline the choice that makes the sentences correct.

Example: I (<u>sit</u>, set) in the front row during math class.

1.   They are (already, all ready) to proceed with your plans.

2.   The students had no (allusions, illusions) about the new course.

3.   What kind of (stationary, stationery) did you use?

4.   (Between, Among) Jennifer and Pat there is much animosity.

5.   You must wait (a while, awhile) for the answer.

6.   You stood (besides, beside) her husband throughout the trial.

7.   Doris (don't, doesn't) like to work cross word puzzles.

8.   She is planning to (immigrate, emigrate) from Ireland.

9. (Everyone, Every one) is planning to attend the graduation.

10. We will give you our answer in just (a while, awhile).

11. The amount was (fewer, less) than I thought.

12. Is she going to move (farther, further) away?

13. This is certainly different (than, from) what I expected.

14. Please stay (in, into) the room until I come.

15. (Leave, Let) us all go promptly.

16. We shall (precede, proceed) according to his wishes.

17. Don't (raise, rise) your voices.

18. What (advice, advise) shall I give?

19. He still must go a long (ways, way).

20. She will (sit, set) the plants there.

21. (Their, They're) voices were raised in song.

22. This item (proceeds, precedes) that one.

23. (Then, Than) it will be too late.

24. He always acts according to (principal, principle).

25. His actions were (unique, most unique).

Exercise 130

Directions: Underline the correct answer.

Example: (Beside, Besides) Tom, who else is going?

1. Everyone passed the exam (accept, except) Terry.

2. The police (accused, alleged) that he was possibly the robber.

3. His acceptance speech (affected, effected) me very specially.

4. His cough was (aggravated, irritated) by the smoke.

5. The number of students in my class (is, are) too many.

6. Bob was (eager, anxious) about his friend's accident.

7. (Any one, Anyone) can help me sort these papers.

8. (Everyone, Every one) of the students has signed up for the trip.

9. We visited my aunt in Florida for (a while, awhile).

10. Were they (enthusiastic, enthused) over winning the game?

11. There was (fewer, less) food donated this year for the poor.

12. The wheel on his bike is (lose, loose).

13. My little brother is very (healthful, healthy).

14. I (may be, maybe) able to go with you tomorrow.

15. Did he (teach, learn) you the rules of the game?

16. This chapter should (precede, proceed) the last chapter.

17. Can you remain (stationary, stationery) for one minute?

18. We took lunch and (then, than) we left.

19. This artifact is (most unique, unique).

20. The next stop is a long (way, ways) from here.

21. (Their, They're) planning to hold a barbecue for everyone.

22. A number of days (was, were) needed to finish the project.

23. The (affect, effect) of his sermon was extraordinary.

24. The choir was (all ready, already) able to sing that song.

25. I would not (advice, advise) you to leave now.

26. Their conduct in the auditorium (irritated, aggravated) the teacher.

27. Did they (accept, except) your criticisms.

28. His temper (effected, affected) our friendship.

29. The students were (all ready, already) assembled in the auditorium.

30. (Everyone, Every one) of the apples in that box was spoiled.

General Punctuation Rules

The rules for punctuation in this textbook are taught where they occur logically. Some general rules, however, are included here as a resource for composition writing. Any material already covered in this text will not be included here.

Commas

1. Use commas between items in a series.

    > Her friend was talented, poised, and beautiful.

2. Use commas after introductory material.

    > Yes, I will be at the meeting.

    > Please, I want you to come now.

    > Early in the morning on a spring day, (prepositional phrases of four or more words)

3. Names of people being addressed.

    > Yes, Mother, I will prepare dinner.

4. When a name is followed by one or more titles, use a comma after the name and after each title.

    > Sally Prendergast, Ph.D., lectured on child development.

5. Use commas with places, dates, and titles.

> On July 12, 1991, we moved to Chicago, Illinois.
>
> On July 4, 1884, the Statue of Liberty was officially presented to the United States.

6. With numbers of more than three digits, use a comma after every third digit from the right.

> 3,400
>
> 23,400
>
> 237,400
>
> 1,237,500

Capitalization

1. Capitalize the names of ships, planes, monuments, awards, and any other particular places, things, or events.

> The Constitution   ship
>
> Lincoln Memorial   monument
>
> Purple Heart   award

2. When a title is used instead of a noun in direct address, it should be capitalized.

> Is that operation very serious, Doctor?

3. Capitalize all words referring to a deity.

> God   Lord   Almighty

Quotation Marks

A direct quotation is a person's exact words or thoughts, and must be enclosed in quotation marks.

> The teacher said, "I will be retiring in June."

An indirect quotation reports only the general meaning of what a person said and does not require quotation marks.

> She said that she would be retiring in June.

Always place a comma or a period inside the quotation marks. Begin the quotation with a capital letter.

> Mary said, "I will go with you tomorrow."
>
> "Class has started," the teacher said.

When a quotation is divided into two parts by an interrupting expression, the second part begins with a lowercase letter.

> "Whatever goals you set for yourselves," the teacher said, "can be achieved."
>
> "When the bell rings," the teacher said, "please leave the room quietly."

When there are two sentences, the second sentence must begin with a capital letter.

> "Everyone is going to the game," he said. "Be sure to bring plenty to eat."

He said, "Everyone is going to the game. Be sure to bring plenty to eat."

Question Marks

The question mark always follows the question and is in front of the quotation mark.

> "When do you plan to finish that assignment?" the teacher asked.
>
> Jennifer asked, "Where shall I put this coat?"

If the quote is not a question, then the question mark goes after the quotation mark.

> Have you ever read the poem "The Tiger"?

The name of the poem is not a question.

> Who said, "Give me liberty or give me death"?

Use quotation marks for short stories, poems, articles from magazines, or anything that cannot be published separately.

> Edgar Allan Poe wrote "The Raven."
>
> The article, "Are We Educating Properly?" should be read by all teachers.

Underline anything that can be published separately: movies, novels, magazines, TV shows, etc. Underline names of paintings, boats, and ships.

> Do you get the <u>Times</u> each week?
>
> Have you ever read <u>The Street Lawyer</u> by John Grisham?
>
> We went to see the movie <u>Titanic.</u>
>
> The movie <u>To Kill a Mockingbird</u> is based on the novel.

Exercise 131

Directions: Rewrite the following sentences with correct capitalization.

Example: Last weekend I saw notre dame play michigan.
Last weekend I saw Notre Dame play Michigan.

1. On the fourth of july belk's department store had a sale.

2. Our school is going to play Paraclete high school on Thursday.

3. My brother went to amsterdam to see rembrandt's paintings.

4. She is taking algebra, English, and spanish next semester.

5. Did aunt Grace write you that letter?

6. The greek gods lived on mount olympus.

7. During thanksgiving vacation, we are visiting my aunt in the south.

8. The falcon is a small sailboat.

9. The president of the united states will probably veto that bill.

10. Did you see the new fords and chevrolets at the auto show?

11. We expect aunt Louise and uncle Fred for christmas vacation.

12. The greeks and romans had many gods.

13. The principal speaker was dr. joseph handsen, the former president of barry university.

14. Tomorrow we will travel north to visit the university of scranton.

15. We studied the revolutionary war last week.

16. Have you ever seen the golden gate bridge?

17. Jerry received the junior achievement award.

18. The house of representatives passed the bill, but the senate did not.

19. My father purchased a general electric stove.

20. The new york city planning commission is holding a special meeting for the public.

21. He was planning to visit the northwest this summer.

22. Central high school is holding a wrestling contest.

23. Gerald A. Gavestone, jr., is a professor at Arizona state university.

24. The south has produced some of america's great writers.

25. Jenny's broken leg was set by dr. john buxton.

Exercise 132

Directions: Rewrite the following sentences with correct punctuation and capitalization.

Example: When he asked will the store open. *"When," he asked, "will the store open?"*

1. John's ford a green truck was going north on elm street.

2. My cousin just graduated from fordham university.

3. Where did you put my purse Sally asked.

4. She rented a halloween costume.

5. On may day the seniors of jefferson high school present a may pageant.

6. May I introduce you to mr. hendricks president of the rotary club.

7. I had no idea she muttered that you would play a trick like that.

8. Where did you find that poem I asked.

9. No mr. rogers we do not like your suggestions.

10. Have you ever read the short story The Night the Bed Fell?

11. Besides my brother Al, there are aunt ella aunt sara my grandmother and my grandfather.

12. Helen this is my aunt clara.

13. Among Thomas Edison's 1100 inventions were the phonograph the incandescent light and the motion picture camera.

14. According to greek mythology Paris a young trojan tried to settle an argument among three of the goddesses.

15. Josephine editor of mcCall's was the main speaker at the dinner.

16. Did you ever meet my neighbor Ann Myers a fine golfer I asked.

17. Jane said your answer is correct.

18. Where she asked did you ever find that old overcoat?

19. When you finish your report the teacher said you can leave for your next class.

20. At north cape the northernmost point of europe the sun does not set from the middle of may until the end of july

21. To tell the truth Jan Marie a law student is one of my best friends.

22. Harry on the contrary prefers skiing to soccer.

23. My mother was born on October 26 1886 in pittsburgh pennsylvania.

24. Giants in the Earth is one of my favorite novels.

25. Have you ever heard the opera Madame Butterfly she asked.

Directions: Rewrite the following sentences with correct punctuation and capitalization.

Example: Irish bread is made of flour baking powder baking soda salt sugar and buttermilk.

Irish bread is made of flour, baking powder, baking soda, salt, sugar, and buttermilk.

1. I am sure she said that you know what you're doing.

2. One of the most famous movies ever made is Gone with the Wind.

3. Lightning has always caused fear explained mrs. pierce and many people will not live in a place that has electrical storms.

4. The principal said it will be a close game.

5. It was Emma Lazarus who wrote give me your tired your poor. . . .

6. It is now time she wrote to improve our educational system.

7. We asked our parents may we go to knott's berry farm.

8. Janes locker and desk are truly a mess the teacher complained.

9. Whose book is this Sara asked.

10. Does Miss Jones let you do experiments Sally asked.

11. We watched an outdated movie called mildred pierce on television last night.

12. At the vienna restaurant they serve only german dinners.

13. In high school you study english literature.

14. March Fong was elected californias secretary of state.

15. The principal announced the superintendent is visiting our high school today.

16. As one of her electives Marcia chose computer literacy.

17. Mabel please help me find my little sister Gloria begged.

18. Where did all the children go I asked.

19. Keith my friend won $62345 in an essay contest.

20. Did you ever visit the jefferson memorial I asked.

21. The federal bureau of investigation set up offices near here she said.

22. No I could not find the novel little women I answered.

23. We sailed down the mississippi river last summer I said.

24. My aunt sue lives in the southeast.

25. Yes we are going to visit yosemite park next summer I replied.

Directions: Rewrite the following sentences with correct punctuation and capitalization.

Example: We drove through ohio kentucky and tennessee on our vacation. *We drove through Ohio, Kentucky, and Tennessee on our vacation.*

1.   The superintendent will visit bellmont high school next week.

2.   The old man said please give me something to eat.

3.   My aunt lives in new mexico, I told her.

4.   We traveled north to visit san diego.

5.   Georgia is now an american citizen.

6.   The league of women voters is holding a convention in chicago next week he announced.

7. We are going to the east to visit your cousin, my father said.

8. She is going to study french this summer.

9. We have stated an explorers club at our school.

10. Jon lives on twenty-ninth street.

11. I met former president Ford last summer.

12. Our history class is held in room 301.

13. My father had an old royal typewriter.

14. We are having a book week the librarian announced.

15. We always watch the world series.

16. Did you study the Robert Frost's poem Birches.

17. Where, the teacher asked, are your reading books.

18. By the way I had a letter from senator johnson.

19. I don't know Albert where your sister is.

20. Bernice Silverman a noted writer will give a talk next month.

21. The coach said be sure all your uniforms are clean.

22. Have you she asked been working all summer.

23. The teacher did say complete this lesson at home.

24. I know he said that we can finish this job by Tuesday.

25. Are all the players ready asked the referee.

The material in this section will strengthen your knowledge of the basics of grammar. Study this section carefully. All the material in this section has been covered in the textbook. Work for mastery.

Directions: Look for errors in capitalization, punctuation, or usage. If there are no mistakes, mark *d*.

_____ 1.   a. The Fourth of July is a famous american holiday.
                b. "We want them to be happy," she said.
                c. Have you ever visited England?
                d. No mistakes.

_____ 2.   a. "Where are you going?" she asked.
                b. Not one of the maps were completely correct.
                c. Would you like to climb Mount Everest?
                d. No mistakes.

_____ 3.   a. The mayor is holding a closed meeting.
                b. The senator from massachusetts is now speaking.
                c. I plan to take English, math, and art.
                d. No mistakes.

_____ 4.   a. My mother made some delicious brownies.
                b. "Where should we go tonight"? Bob asked.
                c. Each of these tests has errors.
                d. No mistakes.

_____ 5.   a. No my friend, I will not go with you.
                b. "It's time to take a rest," Jim replied.
                c. Let me help you, please.
                d. No mistakes.

_____ 6.   a. "We are the winners," Paula announced.
                b. Who will take Cindy and he to the game?
                c. Have you ever seen the Grand Canyon?
                d. No mistakes.

_____ 7.   a. Yes, you will receive an A for your talk.
                b. Relaxing at the beach is fun.
                c. Each of the girls was unhappy over working conditions.
                d. No mistakes.

_____ 8.   a. You're too quick to criticize.
                b. Every one left except Tom.
                c. My rose garden is very beautiful.
                d. No mistakes.

_____ 9.   a. All of them are eager to join the team.
                b. Did you hear the bell at 6:00 A.M.?
                c. Irregardless of the consequences, he did not cooperate.
                d. No mistakes.

_____ 10. a. That pair of shoes is the smallest of the two.
b. Were you anxious about your mother's illness?
c. "That was silly of him," admitted Carl.
d. No mistakes.

_____ 11. a. Someone's tennis shoes were left here.
b. Pat remember to bring the sandwiches.
c. I like to study with Mary and her.
d. No mistakes.

_____ 12. a. One of our dogs is ill.
b. She had no answer for the question.
c. I don't want to see no movie.
d. No mistakes.

_____ 13. a. Sally asked, "Where is the food?"
b. The Spanish Club is not represented.
c. He asked his father, "Why are you tired."
d. No mistakes.

_____ 14. a. Jean and her are going to the dance.
b. "Where did you put my shoes?" he asked.
c. Divide the fruit among the students.
d. No mistakes.

_____ 15. a. Of the two, she is the more talented.
b. My father's office was shut down for a day.
c. Columbus Day is next week.
d. No mistakes.

_____ 16. a. Jill's composition is the longest.
b. Did you read the poem "Southern Fun?"
c. We visited Tampa, Florida, last Sunday.
d. No mistakes.

_____ 17. a. Matt goes to Hamilton High school.
b. Joe, help your brother with the dishes.
c. Anyone may apply for the job.
d. No mistakes.

_____ 18. a. We always go to Aunt Ella's for a couple of weeks.
b. Every one of the cars had a defect.
c. I can't attend none of the meetings.
d. No mistakes.

_____ 19. a. Mail this package to the republic of South Africa.
b. Neither of the packages was mailed on time.
c. "Who," she thought, "might that be?"
d. No mistakes.

_____ 20. a. Tuesday, Columbus Day, is a holiday.
b. "Did you find the answers," she asked?
c. We studied the Battle of Gettysburg today.
d. No mistakes.

_____ 21. a. Mrs. Peters, our secretary, is celebrating her birthday today.
b. My brother is staying at the Lanana hotel in Mexico.
c. Please give he and her this book.
d. No mistakes.

_____ 22. a. This heat wave has broken all records.
b. Several of the books were returned.
c. Either of the girls have my permission to leave.
d. No mistakes.

_____ 23. a. Look out for snakes!
b. He couldn't hardly walk to his room.
c. "Will you lend me enough money for the bus?" he asked.
d. No mistakes.

_____ 24. a. Her answer was no different than mine.
b. Come quickly, Ruth.
c. The doorbell just rang.
d. No mistakes.

_____ 25. a. Jack is more intelligent than Jane.
b. Anyone is welcome.
c. Each of the cheerleaders is ill.
d. No mistakes.

Exercise 136

Directions: Look for errors in capitalization, punctuation, or usage. If there are no mistakes, mark *d.*

_____ 1. a. The teacher asked, "Have you ever read "Birches?"
b. No, it is not wise to leave now.
c. Julie, you should judge for yourself.
d. No mistakes.

_____ 2. a. Yes, she was invited to the party.
b. Please leave him go with us.
c. My mother gave away a few of her roses.
d. No mistakes.

_____ 3. a. Everyone of the team received a letter.
b. No one is capable of that error.
c. He couldn't teach his dog any new tricks.
d. No mistakes.

_____ 4. a. The reunion will be held in Dallas, Texas.
b. North America is one of seven continents.
c. By the way how far is it to Cleveland?
d. No mistakes.

_____ 5. a. Each of the students was working hard.
b. You and her should wait for the others.
c. "Where," he asked, "are my glasses?"
d. No mistakes.

_____ 6. a. She wanted to study with Ginny and me.
       b. Yes, you may borrow my computer.
       c. She received $5000 for her efforts.
       d. No mistakes.

_____ 7. a. Ouch! You stuck me with a pin!
       b. "Its time to go," said the guide.
       c. Better luck next time.
       d. No mistakes.

_____ 8. a. "Jump immediately!" ordered the coach.
       b. Math is more interesting than science.
       c. My cousin said "that he was going on a vacation."
       d. No mistakes.

_____ 9. a. The bill was $2500.
       b. We read the article, "All About Eve," in the paper.
       c. The smallest of the four girls made the varsity softball team.
       d. No mistakes.

_____ 10. a. No, you can't study here.
        b. Someones' coat is on the table.
        c. Let's you and me leave now.
        d. No mistakes.

_____ 11. a. The younger of the three boys left early.
        b. One of my cats is sick.
        c. I was anxious about his illness.
        d. No mistakes.

_____ 12. a. Have you ever visited Japan?
        b. Jupiter is a large, strange planet.
        c. Jane played a powerful brilliant game of tennis.
        d. No mistakes.

_____ 13. a. Mars, one of the closest planets, can be seen with the naked eye.
        b. Jane, my sister, is visiting me today.
        c. The shelf with many library books are now too heavy.
        d. No mistakes.

_____ 14. a. No, it was not he in the room.
        b. Ben, please take this package to the post office.
        c. The weather in fact was ideal for a picnic.
        d. No mistakes.

_____ 15. a. It could have been she on the stage.
        b. Mt. Rushmore, a national monument is a tourists' attraction.
        c. Do you like Swiss cheese?
        d. No mistakes.

_____ 16. a. At the store Marlene bought pencils, paper, and tape.
        b. March 12, 1985, was the day they moved to Chicago.
        c. One of the pencils on the desk were broken.
        d. No mistakes.

_____ 17. a. The principal took the excuses from Fred and she.
b. I will take algebra and general science in high school.
c. Don't send the larger of the two packages.
d. No mistakes.

_____ 18. a. The school has many after-school activities.
b. The vote was unanimous.
c. The annual fiesta was held on May 2 1998.
d. No mistakes.

_____ 19. a. Please give the award to Sam and him.
b. Wrestling with the problem and unable to resolve it.
c. Everyone was enjoying the show.
d. No mistakes.

_____ 20. a. A pot of gold is at the end of the rainbow.
b. There are many students studying french and Spanish.
c. She goes to England every summer.
d. No mistakes.

_____ 21. a. Saturday, an unusual name for a girl, won a four-year scholarship to the high school of her choice.
b. Let's you and me visit her in the hospital.
c. Help! My brother is injured!
d. No mistakes.

_____ 22. a. A bottle of olives were broken.
b. We met the president of the student council.
c. Marvin chose Typing II.
d. No mistakes.

_____ 23. a. Why did you do that?
b. He is one of the senators visiting our school.
c. My sister bought an Oriental rug.
d. No mistakes.

_____ 24. a. Wow! What a beautiful corsage!
b. Bob is more talented than his brother.
c. Your leaving for where?
d. No mistakes.

_____ 25. a. It's a little late to enroll in this class.
b. We found that its leg was broken.
c. They blamed him for the shooting.
d. No mistakes.

Directions: Underline the errors in the following sentences and write the correction on the line at the right. If there is no error, write *Correct*.

1. Everyone of the desks was varnished this summer. _____

2. Do you think he will be our next vice President? _____

3. Our Art Teacher, Mrs. Giles, has taught here for ten years. _____

4. Angela announced, "Mother said that dinner is ready." _____

5. Jenny played very good in our school band. _____

6. Our literature book is the heavier book I carry. _____

7. Her cough is worst today. _____

8. My house is the closer of all my friends. _____

9. The first speaker in the debate was me. _____

10. Beside the excellent meals, the hotel provides many types of recreational facilities. _____

11. Between the four of us, we were able to raise the money. _____

12. We have less honor students this year. _____

13. Your car is faster than our's. _____

14. Most of the sandwiches was eaten. _____

15. All of my belongings was burned in the fire. _____

16. Several of the guests were late for the dinner. _____

17. Somebody in the class are wrong about the problem. _____

18. Nothing is worth that sacrifice. _____

19. My sisters car was vandalized. _____

20. Lizzie enjoys Biology and English. _____

21. Will you take this book to the library please. _____

22. Mr. Gillis our superintendent visited the seventh grade classroom.

    _____

23. Jane is a famous Spanish Dancer. _____

24. In England, we visited Shakespeares home. _____

25. My teacher, kind, wise, and compassionate, will not be returning next year.

    _____

Directions: Underline the errors and write the correction on the line at the right. If there is no error, write *Correct*.

1. Do you often read the bible? _____

2. "I think our car has a flat", complained Jim. _____

3. James's house was destroyed in a tornado. _____

4. An ambassador visited Lincoln High school last week. _____

5. We will study the Bill of Rights in our history class. _____

6. We were anxious to visit the Sahara Desert. _____

7. Somebody is responsible for the loss of Saras shoes. _____

8. The teacher asked, "Has anyone read this poem"? _____

9. Which of the two answers is the best? _____

10. Between John, Henry, and me, there are no ill feelings. _____

11. We studied an English Ballad. _____

12. I don't want none of that fruit. _____

13. Bill don't play tennis anymore. _____

14. The best shooter was her. _____

15. Becky looks much better this morning. _____

16. My puppy ran in the kitchen and knocked over a carton of milk. _____

17. Jerry will immigrate from Australia next month. _____

18. To the winners, John and he, trophies will be given. _____

19. She don't know what to say. _____

20. That gadget save a lot of time. _____

21. Whom will be going with you? _____

22. Doctor M. Smith, a surgeon, works to hard for his own good. _____

23. You sure enjoyed that show last night. _____

24. I was real sad about your mother's death. _____

25. Either of the twins are going out for softball. _____

Directions: Underline the errors and write the correction on the line at the right. If there is no error, write *Correct.*

1. Joan sings good. _____

2. Neither of these books have a good story. _____

3. Everyone of these songs carries an inspirational message. _____

4. Betty and her skipped classes for a ball game. _____

5. The papers were their's to begin with. _____

6. Jill made less errors on her paper. _____

7. The culprit was actually her. _____

8. Bill doesn't want nothing to eat. _____

9. Each of the books were ruined. _____

10. Among the two of us, we collected enough money. _____

11. His sister is the smartest girl I know. _____

12. There's plenty money in the bank. _____

13. May be we should leave now. _____

14. We will rest here a while. _____

15. Everyone in the room are tired of hearing him speak. _____

16. A box of matches often cause big fires. _____

17. Coughing will aggravate her sore throat. _____

18. Any one is allowed to attend the concert. _____

19. Jerry don't study enough. _____

20. "Did you see that movie," she asked? _____

21. "Could you take me that chalk? _____

22. Beside Brian, who else can attend? _____

23. Leave us go with you. _____

24. Exercising daily is very healthy. _____

25. The taller of the three girls is Ella. _____

26. Maria maybe able to visit us this summer. _____

27. We would appreciate less music while we work. _____

28. There was no farther evidence. _____

29. Would you please precede to the stage? _____

30. Her stationary has little designs on the margins. _____

Glossary: The Words We Use

Parts of Speech

There are nine parts of speech

noun
a word that names a person, place, thing, or idea
Hint: You can put *the* immediately in front of it.
Sometimes a noun can name an action:

Swimming is fun.

Nouns are used for the subject, the predicate nominative, and all objects (predicate object, direct object, and indirect object).

pronoun
a word that can take the place of a noun or refer to a noun

John saw the rabbit.

He saw it again later.

verb
a word or group of words that express a state of being, an occurrence, or an action
A verb suggests time (*tense* means time).

John *saw* him.

adjective
a word or group of words that describe (modify) a noun or pronoun
Adjectives answer one of these three questions: how many, what kind of, or which one.

The *tall* man is my father.

adverb
a word or group of words that describe verbs, adjectives, or other adverbs
Adverbs answer any one of these five questions: how, when, why, where, or to what extent (how much).

She was walking *quickly*.

conjunction
a word that joins or connects parts of the sentence
We ran to the corner *but* missed the bus.

interjection
a word that usually expresses emotion
An interjection often stands alone.

Oops! I dropped my books.

preposition
a word that occurs before a noun or pronoun and expresses a relationship between it and another noun or pronoun.

I wanted to sit *near* my friends.

expletive
a word added to fill out a sentence
Expletives do not describe or refer to anything, as in the following example:

There is a big mess in the kitchen.

A big mess is in the kitchen has the same meaning; *there* has no real use except to allow a different arrangement of words.

Parts of the Sentence

subject

the part of the sentence that identifies what is being discussed
The subject of the sentence is always a noun or pronoun.

> *Tyrone* lost his hat.

predicate

the part of the sentence that tells what is happening (or did happen or will happen) to the subject, or what the subject does (or did, or will do)

> His brother *is looking* for it.

complete subject

the part of the sentence that includes the subject and all the words connected to the subject

> *My oldest brother* studied the problem for a long time last night.

simple subject

the main word of the complete subject

> My oldest *brother* studied the problem for a long time last night.

complete predicate

the part of the sentence that includes the verb and all the words connected to the verb

> My oldest brother *studied the problem for a long time last night.*

simple predicate

the verb

> My oldest brother *studied* the problem for a long time last night.

predicate noun (nominative)

the part of the sentence that completes the verb with a word that refers to the subject and *renames* it

> The rose is a *flower*.

predicate adjective

the part of the sentence that completes the verb, refers to the subject and *describes* it

> The rose is *red*.

direct object

the part of the sentence that completes the *action* of the verb and answers the question *what*

> She gave the *book* to me.

indirect object

the part of the sentence that tells to or for whom (or what) something was done

> She gave *me* the book.

Other Terms

antecedent

the noun to which a pronoun refers

> *Jeff* turned off his radio. The pronoun *his* refers to Jeff

sentence

a group of words that express a complete thought
A sentence must contain a subject and predicate.

> *We won the game.*

clause	a group of words that contains a subject and predicate but does not always express a complete thought *if we win the game*
appositive (apposition)	a word or words that rename the noun they follow Appositives help to explain the noun. Jane, *my sister,* is in the seventh grade.
phrase	a group of words that are connected and work together like a single word We got up early *in the morning.* *In the morning* is a phrase that works like an adverb. It answers the question when. Because it begins with a preposition, it can be called a prepositional phrase. Because it works like an adverb, it can be called an adverbial phrase.
modify, modifier	words used to describe the work of adjectives and adverbs Modifiers describe or limit other words. *Some* boys will help.
case	a word used to describe the form of pronouns A single pronoun can be used in three ways and sometimes has three forms. **nominative case:** pronouns used as substitutes for the subject or predicate nominative (*I, you, he, she, it, we, they, who*) **objective case:** pronouns used as substitutes for an object (*me, you, him, her, its, us, them, whom*) **possessive case:** pronouns used to show possession *(my or mine, your or yours, his, her or hers, our or ours, their or theirs, whose)*
voice	a change in the form of a verb that tells whether the subject is acting or receiving the action of the verb
active voice	the subject is acting The hunter *shot* the rabbit.
passive voice	the subject is receiving the action The rabbit *was shot* by the hunter.

The Publisher

Founded in 1970, The Center for Learning is a non-profit educational publisher committed to integrating values and academic learning. A national network of experienced educators write our curriculum units, which are identified by the TAP® (Teachers/Authors/Publishers) trademark. More than 500 English/language arts, social studies, novel/drama, elementary, and religion publications are available for use in public and private schools as well as other educational settings.

These units are regularly evaluated and updated to meet the challenging and diverse needs of teachers and students. Teachers may offer suggestions for the development of new publications or revisions of existing titles by contacting

The Center for Learning

Administrative/Editorial Office
21590 Center Ridge Road
Rocky River, OH 44116
(440) 331-1404
FAX: (440) 331-5414
E-mail: cfl@stratos.net
Web: http://www.centerforlearning.org

For free catalogs describing these units, contact

The Center for Learning

Customer Service Office
P. O. Box 910
Villa Maria, PA 16155
(724) 964-8083 or (800) 767-9090
FAX: (888) 767-8080